INVISIBLE WALLS

INGEBORG HECHT

INVISIBLE WALLS

*A German Family under the
Nuremberg Laws*

Translated by
J. Maxwell Brownjohn

HARCOURT BRACE JOVANOVICH, PUBLISHERS
San Diego   New York   London

Copyright © 1984
by Hoffmann und Campe Verlag, Hamburg
English translation copyright © 1985
by Harcourt Brace Jovanovich, Inc.

Library of Congress Cataloging in Publication Data
Hecht, Ingeborg.
Invisible walls.
Translation of: Als unsichtbare Mauern wuchsen.
1. Hecht, Ingeborg. 2. Jews—Germany (West)—
Hamburg—Biography. 3. Holocaust, Jewish (1939–1945)—
Germany (West)—Hamburg—Personal narratives. I. Title.
DS135.G5H43313   1985   943'.515004924022   85-5870
ISBN 0-15-145317-9
86 000695
Designed by Kate Nichols
Printed in the United States of America

First edition
A B C D E

CONTENTS

DEDICATED TO THE MEMORY OF MY PARENTS—
but written also for my grandsons Matthias and Florian,
whose mother, Barbara, left us in 1977

AUTHOR'S NOTE

LEAFING THROUGH *Das Sonderrecht für die Juden im NS-Staat** was almost like watching a rerun of my early life, half a century after the event. So many aspects of the Third Reich have already been explored that I propose to pick out one theme only—one that has hitherto escaped attention, save in Ralph Giordano's novel *Die Bertinis*, which came out when my manuscript was already complete and on its way to a publisher. My subject is the life of "half-breeds," or "offspring of privileged mixed marriages," in Nazi Germany.

Members of the younger generation are unfamiliar with these abstruse terms and verbal inventions; besides, they have problems of their own. Partly in tribute to those of this persecuted group who died, however, and partly as a contribution

---

*Das Sonderrecht für die Juden im NS-Staat (Special Legislation for Jews in the National Socialist State. A Compilation of Measures and Directives, Their Content and Significance), edited by Joseph Walk, with contributions by Robert M. Kempner and Adalbert Rückert (Heidelberg/Karlsruhe: C. F. Müller Juristischer Verlag, 1981). The decrees cited here may be found, together with relevant references, on the pages indicated.

to the study of modern history, I think it appropriate to document their sufferings.

I have tried to abstain from all personal comments, speculations, complaints, and accusations. This was not easy, least of all in a world where inadmissible comparisons with other, more recent, atrocities are commonplace.

Speaking of comparisons, I have sometimes heard it argued that Hitler made a lot of "Aryan" Germans suffer, too—soldiers and their families, for instance. True, but they suffered as members of the "national community," enjoyed respect and mutual assistance. Their common enemy in battle spoke a different language.

Not so the persecuted, who were treated with scorn, contempt, and unfeeling hostility by people whose language was the same as theirs, and whose community they had belonged to—as fellow Germans—until 1933. The persecuted had to endure suffering as outcasts.

A final word on the subject of the "Special Legislation" decrees. Some of them read so absurdly that one is tempted to burst out laughing, but unintentional comedy on the part of murderers is no laughing matter.

Freiburg, Fall 1983

THE FAMILIES
(1883–1933)

3.24.38: *Jews are not permitted to consult public records except for genealogical purposes and for the study of Jewish folklore. In cases where the said exceptions apply, it must be ensured that the Jewish user of records is given access only to documents essential to the object of his investigation or research. (P. 219)*

I FOUND PARTICULARS of my ancestry, complete with names and details of social status, in a document case left behind by my father. That I possess these papers at all, neatly filed and photocopied (the originals were destroyed by fire), I owe to the period when Jewish lawyers could no longer style themselves attorneys, only "legal consultants," and were forbidden to have other than Jewish clients. That left my father with little work and a lot of time on his hands. The sole purpose for which he was still permitted to set foot in his old professional haunt, the Civil Justice Building on Sievekingsplatz, was to carry out genealogical research and photocopy what he unearthed there.

On September 24, 1883, a son, Felix, was born to the Jewish businessman Jakob Hecht and his wife Hanna, née Calmann, in the Harvestehude district of Hamburg. Felix was the eldest of five children belonging to a German family that would later be declared German no longer.

On April 23, 1900, a daughter, Edith, was born to Police Superintendent Friedrich von Sillich, a Protestant, and his wife Fredegonde, née Ossenkopp, at Harburg an der Elbe. Edith was the scion of a good, solid German family that would later be termed "Aryan."

Friedrich von Sillich, a captain in the Royal Prussian Army Reserve, was last stationed at the headquarters of the 103rd Infantry Division's field recruiting depot in Meiningen. He died at Sains-Richaumont on April 12, 1918, of a heart attack following an air raid.

Jakob Hecht died at Hamburg in the same year.

Edith von Sillich's childhood was a happy one. As a five-year-old attired in a quaint little sailor outfit, she had good reason to feel proud of her papa when the kaiser visited Harburg in 1905—at 4:40 P.M. on June 19, to be precise—because "he was escorted on his progress through the town by Police Inspector von Sillich, likewise riding in an automobile." Thus the *Harburger Anzeiger*, which even printed a photograph of the occasion.

On Sundays and holidays the family would drive by wagonette to Harburg's "Schwarze Berge," there to lunch at one of the pleasant inns in the woods; or promenade down to the Old Harbor, that little gateway to the world near its mighty Hamburg neighbor, to which it was still linked by steam ferry; or stroll across the majestic Elbe Bridge. Harburg was Prussian in those days, and had yet to be incorporated in Hamburg.

As Edith grew older, she would roam the surrounding hills with her girlfriends and sing to the strains of brightly beribboned guitars. Riding was another of her pastimes, inexpensively pursued on a rather decrepit military charger belonging to Harburg's police force, which her father commanded. On Sundays she would attend St. Paul's Church and sing "Ein' feste Burg ist unser Gott," though its third verse . . . "If the world were filled with devils"—had yet to assume any topical significance. She also knew the synagogue on the corner of Eissendorferstrasse and Knoopstrasse, a place of worship frequented by members of a different religion to which no stigma then attached. Jews had lived in Harburg since 1610, under a charter granted them by William, duke of Braunschweig-Lüneburg.

I mention these things because my mother, pretty little Edith von Sillich, who grew up in a snug, friendly environment dedicated to probity and good faith, never quite grasped what befell her after little more than ten years of marriage.

The von Sillichs of Harburg were enthusiastic collectors of pewter, which they used to buy at the Rembrandthaus, the Hechts' antique shop in the Colonnades at Hamburg, though only on a modest scale because an army captain's pay was meager, and there were debts incurred as a lieutenant to be deducted from it.

Felix Hecht, the proprietor's son, who was sixteen years older than Edith, occasionally helped her with her homework.

When war broke out, Edith volunteered for service as a kitchen and ward auxiliary at the Duke of Meiningen Hospital. She had never intended to become a nurse, but the fatherland had summoned all good citizens to do their patriotic duty. An opportunity to continue this budding career occurred when her father died, so she transferred to a school of nursing in Berlin. In 1919, shortly before she completed her training, Felix Hecht asked her to marry him.

The ceremony took place on May 25, 1920, at "Villa Hanna," otherwise known as No. 7, Frauenthal, near the Alster, with a pastor and a cantor in attendance. That evening everyone celebrated at the Winterhuder Fährhaus and posed for a grand family photograph.

The bridal pair had embarked on what came to be known as a "privileged mixed marriage."

I was born on April 1, 1921, in a private clinic owned by Dr. Adolf Calmann, my grandmother Hanna's brother, at No. 68, Johnsallee. My brother Wolfgang was born two years later, on November 11, 1923.

The Nazi authorities were to coin a special term for the likes of us: "first degree half-breeds." It was for us, whom they ceased to regard as German citizens, that they devised the bulk of the so-called Nuremberg Laws "for the protection of German blood and German honor."

No. 7, Frauenthal, named Villa Hanna after my beautiful grandmother, was a handsome corner house with a gabled roof, a portico, and a front garden. It was the one house in this small street in Hamburg's former monastic quarter that did not survive the war. Today its site is occupied by a gas station.

Villa Hanna was situated in Harvestehude, one of the city's finest residential districts, where town houses were adorned with Jugendstil porticoes, neoclassical windows and balconies, neobaroque gables, imposing Wilhelminian façades, and other architectural embellishments typical of the age of German industrial expansion. In the midst of this desirable area was Eichenpark, where we used to feed the swans on the Alster.

The Hecht grandparents and their five children were fortunate to live in Harvestehude. Their forebears had come from the Yiddish-speaking ghettos of Eastern Europe, a vanished world known to us only through the books of Joseph Roth, Isaac B. Singer, and Manès Sperber. Destroyed by deportation and extermination, its sole memorial a few old photographic records, it has passed into history.

But my grandparents were no longer part of that world.

Not until it was engulfed by the common experience of suffering in Auschwitz, Maidanek, Treblinka, and Warsaw were the eastern and western children of Israel reminded of their common roots.

As they relaxed in the handsome garden of their Frauenthal mansion, or on its terrace, which must have been little less spacious than an entire house in one of the eastern ghettos, these "western" Jews were able to forget and dismiss the tribulations of their race—but only very briefly. It was not until the middle of the nineteenth century, or 1864, that Jews were at long last granted full citizenship; only a generation later, they were brutally ostracized once more.

The eldest son, my father, was made to study law. His real love was ancient languages, but Grandfather Hecht wanted a business manager. As things turned out, he might just as well have dispensed with one. . . .

The two younger brothers, Hellmuth and Edgar, were earmarked to take over the family firm and become art dealers. (Hellmuth later emigrated to Quito and became a monk, and nothing more was ever heard of him.) A third brother died in Hamburg at a very early age—the only member of his generation (discounting the monk, one presumes) to have died a natural death. Aunt Alice, a polio victim with a permanent limp, moved to Berlin and ran the Tauentzienstrasse branch of the family firm until it was driven out of business.

In 1927 my father decided to quit the shelter of Grandmother Hanna's luxurious but matriarchal abode. Cashing in his patrimony, he used it to purchase No. 73, Hochallee, a house typical of the area bounded by Klosterstern and Innocentiastrasse. It had a modest neoclassical frontage but none of the ornamentation and architectural flamboyance of tree-lined Frauenthal.

Here Wolfgang and I grew up, and here we went to school, I to a private junior high school for girls in nearby Mittelweg, he to a primary school in Schlüterstrasse. It was in this "respectable" neighborhood between Jungfrauenthal and Hallerstrasse that we played Indians and trappers, learned to bicycle in the then almost traffic-free streets, and hauled our toboggans to Innocentia Park. Our back garden boasted a pear tree big enough to clamber around in—quite an adventure for city-bred children—and a sand pit in which we dug a sort of cavern lined with planks and shrouded in blankets. This was where we smoked pipes of peace—imaginary ones, of course—in the company of Lux the German shepherd, Blacky the cat, and a neighbor's son from nearby Parkallee, who played with us until he joined the Hitler Youth. But we weren't allowed to sleep in the open like the boy next door, whose enviably romantic privilege it was to camp outside with his father for a whole week after Yom Kippur, the Day of Atonement, in memory of the Israelites' trek through the desert. In accordance with religious tradition, which prescribed that the stars should be visible through the roof of their bivouac, they slept in a "tabernacle" of woven twigs. They didn't do this "just for fun," our parents assured us, but our ignorance of Jewish customs extended to the menorah in Father's study, which we simply regarded as a candlestick with seven branches.

Although our parents belonged to different religions, and it was intended that we should someday choose our own, we were told nothing about Judaism. This, I suppose, was an aid to the assimilation to which most "western" Jews aspired.

After we had spent five years as "children from a good home," complete with cook and nursemaid, our parents filed for divorce. Their divorce, which was granted in 1933, had nothing to do with the ominous political situation, nor did they ever quarrel in our presence. They parted for purely personal reasons and on genuinely good terms, as my mother repeatedly demonstrated with a courage and fortitude that later put her own life in danger. One immediate token of this was her refusal to allow my father, who wasn't the most practical of men, to look for another place to live. For the time being, we all remained under the same roof.

PROFESSIONAL WORRIES
AND DOMESTIC UPHEAVALS
(1934–1938)

1.16.34: *Professional contact with attorneys whose license has been revoked, inter alia when revoked on account of non-Aryan descent, is prohibited. This prohibition also extends to the sharing of office facilities, leasings. . . . All sharing of office facilities and professional association between Aryan and non-Aryan attorneys . . . is prohibited. (P. 68)*

12.20.34: *Former attorneys may no longer style themselves "attorney." (P. 100)*

12.19.35: *The courts must ensure that Jews are not designated as public defenders, court-appointed counsel, bankruptcy trustees, and the like. (P. 147)*

BY THE EARLY SUMMER of 1933, decrees and directives like the following had reared their heads everywhere, and the attitude they exemplified was steadily hardening.

5.17.33: *Medicaments of Jewish manufacture are to be prescribed only when other preparations of the same standard are unobtainable. (P. 23)*

6.30.33: *National Socialists are forbidden to enter premises frequented by Jews. This applies only to cafés and restaurants, not to hotels. (P. 34)*

5.9.33: *All municipal employees are requested to desist from patronizing Jewish stores, and to cancel existing monthly credit accounts forthwith. (P. 21)*

The logical effect of these measures was something we still remember as "the boycott."

On April 1, my twelfth birthday, SA storm troopers stationed themselves outside every Jewish store in Hamburg (and elsewhere) and tried to dissuade shoppers from entering. "This is a Jewish-owned business," they announced. "Didn't you know?" Though rather bemused and surprised, plenty of townsfolk were sufficiently unintimidated—at that juncture—to run the Brownshirts' gauntlet and go inside. The situation was too novel and absurd, too unwonted and sudden an encroachment on their daily lives, for them to take a serious view of the threat and what it portended. The very few people to take it seriously were those who had read *Mein Kampf*. After all, Hitler had made no secret of the ruthlessness with which he intended to execute his grand design.

Having found a silver five-mark piece among my birthday presents, I decided to spend a small proportion of my wealth on some chocolate eggs. Outside the local candy store, the men in brown said their piece. My "Jewish kinship" was not apparent—according to the Nazis, all Jews had hooked noses!—so I proudly brushed past them. (At that early stage we could still afford to look proud of our daring; later on, we took such risks with a pounding heart. . . .) The longtime owners of the candy store, two little old ladies, were red-eyed with weeping. I got my chocolate eggs and a marzipan egg as a bonus.

An announcement published the following April gave some indication of how the fatherland proposed to reward its Jewish sons for services rendered:

4.19.34: *According to the* Hamburger Fremdenblatt, *the Aryan Clause applies to all organizations affiliated to the Central Committee of Hamburg's civic associations. Non-Aryan members are to be expelled by 5.15.34. (P. 78)*

I don't know if my father was due for expulsion, but he certainly didn't wait to find out. He had been a member of the

Greater Hamburg Home Guard, Harvestehude District—in other words, an auxiliary policeman—since 1923.

The laws affecting my father's profession came into being before he had really managed to get his practice off the ground, so they nipped his livelihood in the bud. My mother tried to keep the wolf from the door by converting our Hochallee home into a miniature boarding house.

Where our "Aryan" grandparents were concerned, Wolfgang and I occasionally dipped into the Almanach de Gotha, or directory of noble families. It transpired that the Sillichs had not been granted their coveted "von" until 1871. "True" aristocrats, most of whom could trace their lineage back to the Middle Ages, tended to look down their noses at such upstarts. Although we couldn't have cared less whether the "von" was ancient or modern, the little prefix now came in handy. Mother reverted to her maiden name so that "Aryans," too, need have no qualms about renting rooms from us—to begin with, at least—but it soon dawned on us children that our future mode of existence would be a frugal one. Mother had absolutely no idea how to run a boarding house. The place was managed on very haphazard lines, and all that kept our tenants content was the pleasant atmosphere that reigned there. The venture was doomed from the outset, and the strain told increasingly on our parents' state of health.

Domestic dramas were commonplace, most of our tenants being Jewish and under intense emotional pressure, so my father became a sort of unofficial divorce lawyer. One day we were told that Herr and Frau L. had decided to part. The wife and children were to emigrate, the husband would stay behind with us. Everything had been settled amicably, and there was even a farewell party. I can still hear the sentimental lyric blaring from the phonograph horn: "Reich mir zum Abschied noch einmal die Hände, / Goodnight, goodnight, good-nigh-eet. . . ." The ladies dabbed their eyes. Herr L. looked despondent. "From *Viktoria und ihr Husar*—how apt!" my father remarked with a ghost of a smile. The operetta was set in Hungary, and the attractive divorcée was about to join a Hungarian lover abroad. The margin between mawkishness and despair was slender indeed. . . .

But none of these legal tangles helped to improve our financial position, which continued to deteriorate. Having no reserves left to fall back on, my parents were forced to let their staff go.

My mother, though conscientious and courageous, was no businesswoman. On November 29, 1934, the Hochallee house was compulsorily sold at auction and we moved into an apartment at No. 27, Hagedornstrasse. Father came, too. Two of the apartment's six rooms were let to provide us with the barest basic income.

At the same time, Father was obliged to dissolve his partnership, give up his shared office, and dismiss the "Aryan" secretary who had been with him for years. She felt as bad about this as we did, and continued to pay us social calls for a long time to come. Father took a much smaller office in the Hamburger Hof, on Jungfernstieg, and employed a Jewish secretary for a few hours each week.

One of our rooms in Hagedornstrasse was let to a married couple, both of whom were half-Jewish. The young wife, Manon, became like an elder sister to me. She later moved back to Berlin, her native city, where I happened to be staying with her on Kristallnacht, the "Night of Broken Glass." The other rented room was occupied by a Jewish chemist from London, Dr. Herbert Weil, who was working at Hamburg University. Both of them subsequently testified to the postwar Reparations Office that we were still, at this time, in possession of "intact, middle-class household effects." Such were the lengths to which one was driven in the 1950s by officialdom's strange insistence on proof that was almost impossible to obtain. . . .

The apartment was, in fact, quite well appointed in a way that recalled my grandparents' luxurious establishment on Frauenthal, though the furniture was beginning to fall apart. We did not, however, have enough to live on. After school I acted as baby-sitter for five precious marks a week—a rather unusual sideline in those days, and one I heartily disliked.

But even this apartment, with its faded elegance, its balcony and garden, was not to be ours for long. In 1937 we moved again, this time to Hansastrasse, where we took an apartment somewhat at odds with our customary way of life. We shared the place with a couple whom we had never met before. Herr S. and his wife—he was a baker—occupied one and a half rooms; we occupied the remaining three and a half. It was, to say the least, an unfamiliar situation.

This time Father did not accompany us. He stayed behind in Hagedornstrasse with his younger brother Edgar, who, together with Aunt Hanna and cousin Hans, had been our neighbor there. Edgar's existing tenant, an "Aryan" art dealer named Alfred Lawrenz, or "Ali" for short, made room for Father by moving in with us. This was a blessing. Ali proved a great source of help in the dark days ahead. But for him, we should not have survived the coming years so relatively unscathed.

THE "COMRADES"
(1934-1936)

8.17.34: *Young persons belonging to Jewish youth clubs, who do not participate in State Youth Day, may go hiking on Sundays but are not permitted to engage in athletics. (P. 89)*

10.8.35: *Hostels constructed or still to be constructed by Jewish youth clubs will henceforth bear the designation "Jewish overnight centers," not "Jewish youth hostels." (P. 135)*

In 1934 a school friend roped me into the "German Jewish Comrades' Hiking Association." This club sported a smart pennant—a white seagull on a blue background—and a snappy marching song: "Comrades one and all are we, decent types we aim to be. . . ."

It was through the association that I got to know "Little Inge" (a nickname that differentiates her from my lanky self to this day), whose fate will accompany me through these pages as it has throughout my life. Our name was popular in those days, not least with assimilated Jews, because it sounded so irreproachably Nordic. Little Inge was fair-haired and blue-eyed, which made her an exception in our group. "And she claims to be half-Jewish!" said one of the boys when she first turned up. "Hitler and Goebbels would be madly envious of your 'master race' looks." We were becoming adept at black humor, and Little Inge's appearance gave rise to a lot of tragicomic incidents.

For two years we spent our Sundays and vacations tramping through the hills outside Harburg and southward across the Lüneburger Heide to Hittfeld, Buchholz, and Müden.

Because we didn't regard ourselves as a specifically "Jewish" association, we ventured into youth hostels—not always without a trace of uneasiness—and joined other hikers in the dining hall or around the campfire until our beloved club was disbanded in 1936.

Evening meetings were held once a week. It was some time before our parents gathered, from certain out-of-character remarks and snippets of jargon, that our group leaders had begun to subject us to "sociopolitical" indoctrination. Actually, it bored us stiff when they felt duty-bound to read us extracts from *Das Kapital*, and well-meant exegeses of Marxism from older comrades did little to set us on the leftward road, though we naturally shared their devotion to justice for the oppressed of this world. Our unfortunate parents were now doubly afraid, however, not that we would develop Red Front tendencies, but that our association might be branded Communist as well as Jewish and hounded in consequence.

The hitchhiking and singing we enjoyed. Hitchhiking was a far less common mode of travel than it is today—far less potentially dangerous, too. We always hitchhiked as a group, cadging rides from friendly truck drivers and bellowing our songs into the wind, which made the white seagull on our blue pennant flap and flutter overhead. To good little middle-class girls, it all seemed the height of adventure. Despite the ludicrous decree of August 17, 1934, we also took part in field sports and scouting. For once, I wasn't too annoyed with the authors of such bizarre edicts, because I found violent physical exertion in the woods and fields intolerable as well as unnecessary. "Growing too fast for her heart to cope" was the verdict of "Uncle Dr. Zacharias," our longtime family physician and friend, when swimming proved to be the only sport I could stand.

It should here be added that Dr. Zacharias was deported

to Theresienstadt on July 15, 1942. I came across one last, pathetic reminder of him in Käthe Starke's book *Der Führer schenkt den Juden eine Stadt,* which appeared in 1975. Having contracted typhus, he took his own life. "He had chosen not to wait until malnutrition completed its work. In view of prevailing conditions, he put an end to himself. On August 11, 1942, three weeks after his arrival, this gifted physician . . . and expert diagnostician made his own diagnosis and acted on it by taking a drug he had brought with him."

On Mondays we waged verbal warfare with the BDM [German Girls' League] members in our class. Half the pupils in our school were Jewish, and since friendships were still unaffected by racial mania, our debates did not assume a very dramatic form. After all, we sang the same songs in praise of the great outdoors, with their allusions to sun, wind, and stars. Only the very latest brand of doggerel failed to appeal to us: "As the golden sun of evening / Sent its last rays slanting down, / One of Hitler's regiments / Marched into a little town. . . ." Pity to spoil a good tune, we thought.

In 1936 the Comrades' Hiking Association was banned. The Zionists among us, well aware that there was only one place on earth where a Jewish community could try to find peace, were all for emigrating to Palestine. The Communists wanted to stay, if possible. Arrested and detained for some time, our group leader was released before long because his family had hurriedly made arrangements for him to emigrate. However, we now knew what a concentration camp was. . . .

Little Inge and I were the only girl comrades left. Our fathers, having fought for Germany in the war, were deluded enough to bank on the gratitude of a country that had disowned them. Decrees like the one below show just how mean and cynical the authorities could be when they chose:

7.13.36:   *Concessionary telephone calls for war-blinded veterans will not be granted to non-Aryans. (P. 168)*

Though keen on sports, unlike me, my brother Wolfgang was soon expelled from the Hamburg Athletic Club (HSV)—a blow from which he took a long time to recover.

His enthusiasm for football had prompted him to hitchhike to Berlin for the 1936 Olympics. This was a rare mode of travel, as I have already said, and thirteen-year-olds were not as sophisticated as they are today, but my parents, who could not afford to pay his fare, had neither the heart nor the strength of mind to deny him such an important and exceptional treat.

Nazi opportunism during the games was reflected in confidential directives like these:

6.11.35:   *Notices reading "Jews Unwelcome" and the like are to be unobtrusively removed (on account of the Olympic Games) from all main thoroughfares. (P. 117)*

12.3.35:   *To avoid jeopardizing the 1936 Olympic Games in Berlin, all anti-Jewish placards and posters in the vicinity of Garmisch-Partenkirchen, where the Winter Games will be held, are to be removed. (P. 143)*

My brother also had religious interests and commitments. He belonged to the "Vereinigung 1937" [1937 Confraternity], originally registered as the "Reichsverband nichtarischer Christen" [National Association of Non-Aryan Christians] and later as the "Paulusbund" [League of St. Paul]. The Paulusbund, too, organized excursions and hiking tours and held evening get-togethers, but the Gestapo had to be notified of all such meetings in advance. This was less an incentive than a deterrent, and the league was banned before the outbreak of war.

24

The thwarting of Wolfgang's enthusiasms, religious and athletic, made life almost more difficult for him than it was for me. As the forcible estrangement of "Aryans" and "non-Aryans" proceeded with awful inevitability, so more and more mental conflicts arose. Wolfgang became very silent, very withdrawn, and this was bound to affect his outlook on life.

SCHOOL DAYS
(1935–1937)

9.15.35: Law for the Preservation of German Blood and German Honor

1. Marriages between Jews and nationals of German or kindred stock are prohibited. Marriages contracted despite this are null and void.

2. Extramarital intercourse between Jews and nationals of German or kindred stock is prohibited.

3. Jews may not employ in their households female nationals of German or kindred stock aged less than forty-five years. (P. 127)

9.15.35: Reich Citizenship Law

Only nationals of German or kindred stock are citizens of the Reich. Political rights are vested in Reich citizens alone. (P. 127)

11.14.35: Executive Order Pertaining to the Reich Citizenship Law

Jews (i.e., persons descended from at least three racially full-Jewish grandparents, full-Jewish being taken to mean belonging to the Jewish religious community, or half-breeds with two full-Jewish grandparents . . .) cannot be citizens of the Reich, have no right of political franchise, and may not hold public office. . . . The Führer can grant exemption from these regulations. (P. 139)

MY BROTHER AND I were twelve and fourteen years old respectively when the Nuremberg Laws were promulgated, so we had at least some idea of what they meant. My realization of the terrible fears they must have aroused in my parents, whose "privileged mixed marriage" had produced two "half-breeds," I owe to Lotte Paepcke, who presented me with a copy of her book *Ich wurde vergessen* when it was published in 1970. Born at Freiburg in 1910, she qualified as a lawyer in 1933 but was then debarred from practicing, either independently or at the university.

4.6.33:   Junior Staff Regulation

> *The filling of junior faculty posts with members of the Jewish race is prohibited; existing contracts of employment with such persons must not be extended or renewed. (P. 11)*

Lotte Paepcke was shielded from further danger by her marriage to an "Aryan" scientist, but not indefinitely. When her position became precarious, she went into hiding in a Freiburg

29

convent. To begin with, however, she and her family lived in Leipzig. Their neighbors in the apartment house there, who had to be informed of her status, accepted her and were not unfriendly toward this "mixed" couple, whom they regarded as faintly exotic, but the price that had to be paid for their goodwill was high indeed.

"I cleaned the stairs and corridors with the utmost diligence . . . and greeted all those strangers in an affable, ingratiating manner. There it was again, looming over me, the curse that weighed so heavy on the persecuted: the need to beg for benevolence. . . ."

For her life between two worlds was a mosaic composed of fragments which, when put together, could not be other than a picture of self-effacing discretion. She puts it this way:

"You had to bamboozle all the people you encountered into liking you, so as to disarm them in an emergency. You had to work on them surreptitiously so that, whatever happened, their compassion would be primed and ready, for example, to mitigate the lust for hatred ordained by the authorities."

Although the other tenants had accepted Lotte Paepcke and her family, a member of the Nazi women's association was detailed to "ensure that the Jewess behaves decently, see that she causes the neighbors no offense, and note her associates." One need hardly point out how easy it would have been for someone living in an apartment house to wrangle with a neighbor over some trifle and thus "cause offense," but the persecuted cannot afford such luxuries. "The outcast's weapon was to be likeable."

Lotte Paepcke's son Peter presented an even more dramatic problem. He was eight years old.

"When his father entered him for the relevant primary school, the headmaster, a holder of the Nazi 'Blood Order,' did not disguise his reluctance to admit a half-breed. Although

Peter was debarred from a secondary education, however, the primary school was obliged to accept him. So he was duly subjected to German discipline, coming to attention and saluting every morning when the monitor reported that Class IIIb had 'fallen in' for lessons, and marching around with the others in rank and file during break. Only the monitor at their head was entitled to salute assistant teachers, whereas the headmaster had to be smartly saluted by everyone in the school. Peter learned that the Führer never slept a wink, so great was his concern for his people, and that Jews should be struck whenever one came across them. He communicated this advice to us at supper one evening. The blood rushed to my head, I was so appalled by the enormity of the moment and my inability to say, 'Look, here's a Jew sitting right in front of you—your own mother!' But the boy was still so childish and naïve and so inclined to blurt out everything he knew that we didn't dare enlighten him. . . . I was filled with shame. My life was becoming diseased with simulated friendliness, breaking out in sores produced by the bacillus of insincerity. Many were the nights when I debated whether to wield the scalpel and come clean, with the child and everyone else. Any such operation was bound to be fatal, however, and I was driven to conclude that it would be more courageous to go on enduring the pain of dishonesty with a view to saving the whole situation. And so I felt myself taking on the look in the eye, the obsequious smile, that has accompanied the Jews on their millennial progress through the lives of alien peoples."

Unlike me, Little Inge can recall exactly when she first heard of the Nuremberg Laws. She was with her class at Vogelkoje, the school's vacation hostel on the island of Sylt.

"One night we were all instructed to assemble in the dining hall. Some Nazi bigwig was sounding off on the radio—Goebbels, I think. He was proclaiming the 'Nuremberg Laws.' I heard, 'For the preservation of German blood and German honor . . .' We weren't really concentrating, and would much sooner have been doing something else. My form mistress, Fräulein Riecke (who's still alive and has always been a resolute anti-Fascist), became more and more edgy. After pacing up and down, she paused behind my chair. As though by chance, she rested one hand on my shoulder, then momentarily stroked my hair. I was rather puzzled, because I hadn't grasped the significance of the announcement and the extent to which it would affect my future, my whole life. That wasn't made clear to me until I got home. My parents were waiting for me at the station, and my father, who was usually so cheerful and full of fun, greeted me with a funereal expression."

There were BDM girls in Little Inge's class, too.

"After the Sylt trip, one or two of them started making remarks about my 'non-Aryan' ancestry. When Fräulein Riecke heard this, she asked me to leave the classroom a moment. Then she impressed on the others that I didn't belong to one 'side' or the other—that I'd fallen between two stools, so they must treat me fairly and decently, not cut the ground from under my feet. My classmates were impressed by her powers of persuasion. The rest of the teachers at our school were also firmly opposed to Hitler, so I was able to complete my final year and take my junior high school diploma with a pleasurable sense of security, surrounded by loyal friends with whom I still keep in touch to this day. I wasn't allowed to take my university entrance examination, but that would have been financially impossible in any case, because my father—he was a leather merchant, and no 'Aryan' firm could do business with him—was finding it harder and harder to make a living.

"Shortly before the junior diploma exam in April 1937, our class began to receive sporadic visits from officials sent by the high school inspectorate. One of these preliminary oral examinations was in English, a subject I excelled at, so I often got asked questions. At the staff meeting afterward, the official asked Fräulein Riecke who I was, describing me as 'that archetype of the Aryan race.' With the greatest relish, she informed him that I was the only 'half-Jewess' in her class."

Inge's sister Ursula, who was four years younger, fared less well. She had to leave the Emilie Wüstenfeld School after only two years because it was scheduled to be made "Jew-free," so she failed to complete her education. Strangely enough, though, she was deemed worthy of employment in an "Aryan" household during her year's compulsory national service. Then, after attending a private business college, she went to work in an office. This meant that she had, by a roundabout route, ended up in a job as good as we, with our junior high school diplomas, could still hope to obtain.

From 1927 onward I had attended the Ria Wirth School, a private establishment on Mittelweg. We were in the fifth year when Fräulein Angerstein became our form mistress. The need to impart "National Socialist ideas" wrought an inevitable change in the teaching of her two special subjects, German and history. We greatly admired her, however, and I was saddened rather than angered by her habit of wearing a swastika pin in her blouse. Perhaps it was her way of forestalling any official rebukes for her willingness to teach at so racially mixed a school.

Aware that I enjoyed writing and reading, but that I prided myself on the length of my German compositions, Fräulein Angerstein taught me that brevity is the soul of wit. She showed me how an author could be both discursive and "masterly" by introducing me to the works of Adalbert Stifter. We read *Brigitta* together, and she also presented me with a copy of *Abdias*.

One day she asked me why I didn't attend one of the so-called national-political classes at which pupils were familiarized with "the Germany of today," adding, "You're just as much half-Aryan as half-Jewish, aren't you?" So I turned up, just for once, and heard my intelligent, well-respected teacher spouting Nazi slogans. Did she really believe such rubbish, I wondered? Well, even if I couldn't skip the ridiculous daily "flag parades" in the little school yard, I could at least pass that up.

7.30.34: *Exemption of non-Aryan pupils from attendance at weekly classes in "National Socialist ideas" (national political instruction) held on Saturdays for pupils who do not belong to the Hitler Youth. Non-Aryan pupils are to be excused from these on request. (P. 87)*

Our headmistress joined the NS-Frauenschaft [National Socialist Women's Association] and started to treat her Jewish and half-Jewish pupils with a certain aloofness. This, too, may have been a form of protective camouflage, because she never asked any of them to leave. She did need fee-paying parents, of course, but I shall always be grateful to her for granting me a scholarship during my latter years at the school, when we could no longer meet the substantial cost of a private education. If she sometimes saw fit to point out that my special circumstances obliged me to make a special effort, showing little awareness of the childish distress occasioned by such a sense of obligation, this was only secondary to the problem I shared with so many other girls: how were we supposed to concentrate in school when things were so bad at home?

Elisabeth Flügge, a teacher whose subjects included German, local studies, geography, mathematics, botany, and zoology, was made of different stuff. Employed at the school since 1926, she steadfastly refused to trim her sails to the winds of change. With a courage that only her contemporaries can fully appreciate, she devoted herself to the welfare, not only of her bewildered and apprehensive pupils, but also of their gravely endangered parents. She never forgot the occasion in 1933 when one of her girls timidly inquired, "Are *Jewish* children allowed to go collecting, too?" It was a reasonable question, given the hordes of children, both in and out of Hitler Youth uniform, who infested the sidewalks with coin boxes in their hands. In those days, everyone was collecting from everyone else for every conceivable form of charity (Winter Relief Fund, Mother and Child Fund) and on every possible occasion (e.g., "Stewpot Sundays," when the German housewife was officially encouraged to serve up a simple, one-course meal and put the money she saved in a collecting box). Not unnaturally, Jewish children wanted to join in. They had yet to learn the meaning of isolation.

"When you take your girls on an outing," the headmistress had enjoined Frau Flügge, "be sure to put all the blondes in front."

When Jews became subject to a variety of travel restrictions—they were barred from sleepers and dining cars, could only travel third class, and found that many hotels and boarding houses either couldn't or wouldn't take them in—Frau Flügge rented a ten-room house at Ollsen in der Heide and vacationed there with her own two youngsters and a dozen Jewish children. I spent one vacation there myself, as I was recently reminded by her niece Ilse, a school friend of mine. "We swam in the Aue, picked blueberries, played theater," she wrote. "It was a lovely, lighthearted time, don't you remember?"

My memories of it are only vague—blurred and obscured by all the less lighthearted happenings at home. . . .

One day Frau Flügge heard from a Jewish lawyer that the mother of one of her pupils was to be deported. "So I went to the Gestapo with my knees knocking," she told an interviewer from the *Hamburger Abendblatt*. The Gestapo officer reminded her that she was addressing a public servant. "So are you," she retorted, and a miracle occurred. The man behind the desk poured out his heart to her. He'd always tried to do his honest duty, he said despairingly, but now—"Now I'm expected to compile death lists for that devil!" He removed Frau Flügge's protégée from his list, but a colleague later restored her name in line with Party directives.

Frau Flügge also managed to help would-be emigrants in a very special way. She persuaded Lady Oldfield of Cambridge, a friend of her daughter's and niece of Lord Balfour, the former prime minister, to provide affidavits—documents guaranteeing large sureties—for penniless Jews who would otherwise have been refused admission to many countries. Anyone in possession of such a document could consider himself saved.

One long-heralded decree was phrased as follows:

2.24.39:   Obligatory Relinquishment of Jewish-Owned Gems and Articles of Jewelry

> *In regard to the acquisition and purchase of such articles of precious metal, precious stones, and pearls as are to be surrendered by Jews, no offer may henceforth be declined by the same. . . . (P. 283)*

The obligation on Jews to surrender "valuables" of all kinds, including fur coats and objets d'art (the list, which later embraced typewriters, radios, and electrical appliances, was infinitely elastic!), made it hard for emigrants to support themselves

36

in foreign countries, because they could take no money at all. Like other courageous Germans, Frau Flügge began to smuggle valuables abroad with the aid of a friend. On one occasion, jewelry secreted in the funnel of the *Monte Rosa*, a German passenger ship bound for Rio de Janeiro, was picked up there by its owners.

In this as in other respects, Elisabeth Flügge risked her life.

It would be facile to ask why so few—or, at any rate, too few—people summoned up the courage to help the victims of Nazi persecution more effectively. Speaking for myself, I know that I would never have done what Sophie and Hans Scholl, those young German resistance fighters of the White Rose movement, tried to do for all our sakes. They died in 1943, in the cause of freedom, and went to the gallows so bravely that even their jailers and executioners remarked on it.

I say this because the land of Israel has tried to show due gratitude. In the mountains near Jerusalem is the Avenue of the Just, and planted there for Elisabeth Flügge is a little carob tree. It commemorates her receipt of Israel's highest honor, the Yad Vashem medal and citation. Yad Vashem is also the name of the monument erected there in accordance with Isaiah 56:5: "Even unto them will I give in mine house and within my walls a place and a name. . . ." Many millions of stones make up its mosaic floor, one for each of those who were sent to concentration camps and murdered.

Elisabeth Flügge died in Hamburg on February 1, 1983.

Her diametrical opposite was our scripture teacher, a dapper, good-looking clergyman from a neighboring parish. My enthusiasm for the printed word earned me his benevolent interest and the proud privilege of reading aloud to the class.

Then, one day, I noticed that he had begun to ignore me. It wasn't long before I grasped the truth: he had discovered the "ancestry" of the girl he had so often invited to read from the New Testament. I never attended scripture class again.

3.13.35: Segregation of Children of Non-Aryan Descent in Primary Schools

The establishment of separate Jewish primary schools is to be encouraged. The drafting of a law to this effect is in hand. To facilitate racial segregation, school authorities are to compile a statistical analysis of their pupils' racial affiliations. (P. 108)

8.31.35: *Prizes may not be awarded to non-Aryan pupils. (P. 125)*

In contrast to Little Inge and me, my brother Wolfgang suffered detriment and discrimination in primary school, and was denied the opportunity of moving to a junior high school after four years. In 1937 he became a clerical trainee, but he also contrived to attend a private night school and obtain his junior high school diploma—in defiance of discrimination, as it were. (After July 2, 1942, he would have required ministerial permission even for that.)

OUTLOOK UNCERTAIN
(1937–1938)

4.4.34: Restrictions on Attendance at Secondary Schools

Restrictions on the admission of non-Aryan pupils apply not only to secondary schools but also to junior high schools (pursuant to the law against overfilling German schools). As regards admission of non-Aryan pupils to these schools . . . preference must be given to pupils with a proven admixture of Aryan blood. . . . Children of Aryan descent may on no account be disadvantaged in favor of those of non-Aryan descent. (P. 76)

ALTHOUGH "LIMITED OPPORTUNITIES" for advancement existed on paper, it was effectively impossible for us, by the time I left school, to move from junior high schools to secondary, college preparatory schools. We were thus denied the chance to matriculate and go to the university. Older companions in misfortune were just able to graduate, if they had completed their courses by April 1934, but most of them were first required to prove that they would leave the country immediately afterward.

This put an end to my childhood dream, which was to follow in my father's footsteps and study law; in any case, his practice was scarcely worthy of the name by then. I had no time to wallow in despair, however. What mattered was to act fast, before any new regulation could be imposed, and decide on the best thing to do under the prevailing circumstances. If I couldn't be a lawyer, the profession I chose must at least involve the written word. Publishing? Journalism?

In the winter of 1936 my headmistress had sent me to the editorial offices of the *Hamburger Fremdenblatt* with an excellent German report and a letter of recommendation. After a pleasant interview, I was offered a traineeship and given a questionnaire to complete. Elated, I sat down at a little table with pen poised. Then the truth dawned.

"Non-Aryans" were unacceptable. My previous knowledge of the Nuremberg Laws had been only theoretical, so to speak; now their evil, cruel reality was staring me in the face in black and white.

I left the newspaper office and walked across Rathausplatz, which had already been renamed in honor of Germany's great Leader. What pleasure could I take in the splendid neoclassical arcades beside the Kleine Alster—what pleasure could I take in the whole of this lovely, beloved city—if the sense of belonging was denied me? I envied the happy people in the motor launch chugging past below me on its way from Kehrwieder Canal to Jungfernstieg Bridge. With mingled sentimentality and earnestness, I wondered what life had left to offer me. But I never asked myself that question again. It was only later that I grasped how much I managed to endure for twelve long years, though always buoyed up by a feeling of happiness that I lived in Hamburg. I never wished to be anyone or anything else—not even "Aryan."

It was Easter 1937, and our final day at school had arrived. First came a rather emotional lesson with a school inspector listening in, then a speech about our going forth into the big, wide world, then the traditional program of entertainment staged by the class below ours. Then we all repaired to the classroom to make our farewells.

Most of the Jewish girls had already obtained passage on ships bound for freedom, though only after some anxious moments. I particularly recall Steffi Bernstein, a shipowner's daughter, who came to school looking tearful, day after day, because her father had been arrested. (The "Aryanization" of the Hamburg shipping lines plays a part in Arnold Zweig's documentary novel *The Axe of Wandsbek*.)

My "Aryan" classmates were in high spirits. Some of them were going on to senior schools, others entering the professions of their choice.

Neither of these things applied to me. I could neither emigrate nor train for a profession that appealed to me. My father had found me a probationary post with Gustav Weber, a patent attorney with offices at No. 11, Rathausmarkt, but the very term "commercial trainee" grated on my ears. It was just about the last form of vocational training I had hoped for. "Gracious me," said Fräulein Angerstein, who was still sitting there with a handful of stragglers, "anyone would think you were being sent to the scaffold, not out into the world!" My retort dismayed us both. "Maybe I am," I heard myself say, "or are you so sure I'm not?" She was somewhat startled, possibly by the realization of what form my future might take. "You can come and see me anytime," she told me—and I did.

As I made my way slowly out of the big school door through which I had so often raced with only seconds to spare before class, I offered up a silent prayer: "Not yet, please not yet . . ." My father was waiting outside No. 10, Mittelweg, just as he and my mother had waited ten years before with the bag of candies traditionally presented to German children on their first day in school. Despite everything, they had been good years. "Come on," my father said, "let's go and eat."

By this time, everyone was familiar with the "Jews Unwelcome" sign displayed by restaurants, inns, and cafés. Very few eating places had resisted the pressure to conform. One of them was the Vegetarisches Restaurant over the arcades beside the Kleine Alster, another a restaurant beside the elevated railroad station at Hoheluft Bridge. Signor Ferrari's Italian restaurant near the Alstertor also held out for a while. But when he was strongly urged, as a citizen of an Axis country, to put up one of the notices, he eventually did so. Although he allowed us to eat in a back room, our appetite for pasta was spoiled.

The day I left school we lunched at the Vegetarisches. All survivors of the Holocaust know what it is to dream, either of searching vainly for their murdered relatives, or of being reunited with them in pleasant times gone by. Whenever I dream of that lunch, the dream is a pleasant one.

One of our friends was a student of singing named Rainer Bujard. Young though he was, he had had his share of troubles. An "Aryan" with only one parent living, he was lucky enough to have his studies subsidized by Dr. Ascher, a respected Jewish physician who belonged to my parents' circle of acquaintances. Rainer had originally lived, more like a foster son than a lodger, with the doctor's daughter and her children. A few weeks prior to the evening on which he invited us to join him in celebrating my "going out into the world," he had been bullied into moving out by anti-Jewish neighbors who not only browbeat him but threatened his landlady and made the vilest insinuations against her. His new abode was a basement apartment, damp but romantic and inexpensive.

Little Inge had also been invited. "We must celebrate your coming of age!" Rainer insisted. I didn't find this "a consummation devoutly to be wished," but he knew the best way to console me. Seating himself at the piano, he raised his impressive bass voice in an aria from Verdi's *Falstaff*, which he was then studying.

Later we danced to the phonograph. One of the popular

hits of the day was a schmaltzy ballad in which the vocalist yearned to daydream with his or her beloved beneath the palm trees of Monte Carlo. My dearest wish that night would have been to loll beneath a palm tree, as far from Hamburg as possible.

Rainer was killed in the war.

After a year's experience of general office work, I was sick to death of sorting out files and keeping the petty cash. Herr Weber was an ultraconservative gentleman who never mentioned money (either you had it or you didn't), and my trainee's salary of fifteen marks a month—the going rate in those days—was hardly calculated to fire me with professional enthusiasm. This, allied to conditions at home, prompted me to terminate my traineeship.

In October 1938 I landed a so-called beginner's job with Herr Emil Todtmann of Beneckestrasse, a commercial representative dealing in "domestic and foreign alcoholic beverages." His office was in his apartment, and I fared extremely well there. Frau Todtmann, who loved making waffles, supplemented the rather inadequate diet I got at home by giving me hearty breakfasts. She and her husband were a humane, generous, and charitable couple. Herr Todtmann strove hard to overlook my failings in this uncongenial job. When he noticed how often I had trouble with my shorthand, for example, he allowed me to write in longhand. He had to let me go in the fall of 1939. The outbreak of war restricted the Germans to "domestic alcoholic beverages." They imported no more Veuve Clicquot (that was soon available to them in France, free of charge!), only the vermouths manufactured by Italy, their Axis partner, and those my former boss could handle on his own.

In 1954 Herr Todtmann wrote as follows to the Reparations Office: "When I interviewed Fräulein Hecht in 1938, she informed me that she had been obliged to abandon her traineeship after eighteen months in order to assist her parents financially. Her father's practice was steadily shrinking as a result of discriminatory legislation. . . . At the end of 1938 her father was sent to Oranienburg concentration camp and his practice was closed down. The family had a very bad time thereafter, which was why I so often came to their aid."

After the warmth of the atmosphere in Beneckestrasse, my next place of work left me cold. I briefly managed to survive in the Altona office of a construction executive, but only with the help of a cheerful Swedish colleague who taught me to say "Tack så mycket, jag mår bra" (Thanks a lot, I'm fine)—a phrase I often used on her. In January 1940 I became a clerk in a printing house on Hopfenmarkt, in the center of the Old City. The boss, Walter Prunst, put up with a great deal on my account, because summer 1940 was when my parents were arrested and sent to Fuhlsbüttel Prison via city hall, which became a notorious interrogation center. Eager to earn some extra money, I also worked evenings for a nearby chemical business. The managing director, Rolf Sommer, who very soon employed me full time, assisted victims of persecution in his own way. His partner, Dr. Pschorr, had a Jewish wife, and his attorney, Herbert Samuel, who had been articled to my father and became vice-president of Hamburg's municipal parliament after the war, was half-Jewish. Rolf Sommer courageously stood by them in defiance of his chief clerk, who was a Nazi.

I am still in touch with Elly R., who worked with me at this period. To quote from a letter she sent me when she heard

I was writing this book: "I still have a vivid recollection of the timid, dejected way your father came into the office. You urged him not to be scared of me, though, and told him I wasn't dangerous in spite of my swastika pin. I didn't understand at the time. Had I known what I know now, I'd have regarded it as a vile piece of Jew-baiting."

THE
"NIGHT OF BROKEN GLASS"
AND THE
"LAMBETH WALK"
(1938)

11.10.38: Measures to Be Taken Against Jews Tonight

*Immediate preparations and consultations with
police chiefs in attendance. Only those measures
may be taken which carry no threat to German
lives or property. (Synagogues to be burned only
when there is no risk to the surrounding area.)
No Jewish homes or business premises to be destroyed or looted; non-Jewish business premises to
be protected; no Jews of foreign nationality to be
molested. Summary confiscation by the police of
documentary records belonging to Jewish religious
communities. In all districts, as many Jews—
well-to-do Jews in particular—are to be detained
as can be accommodated in the detention centers
available. Upon their request, the appropriate
concentration camp must be contacted forthwith,
so that they can be accommodated there as soon
as possible. All State Police [Gestapo] headquarters are instructed not to intervene by taking
countermeasures. (P. 253)*

THE AUTHORITIES BEGAN to intensify our isolation in a deliberate, methodical way.

11.12.38:   *Jews are forbidden to frequent theaters, movie theaters, concerts, exhibitions, etc. (P. 255)*

That was outrageous enough, but it was very soon followed by a decree enjoining us to surrender our radio sets. With purposeful, insidious ingenuity, the persecuted were being cocooned in their own misery.

My father and I enjoyed going to the movies together, for instance to the Waterloo on Dammtorstrasse, where American films such as *San Francisco* or *Maytime* were premiered until 1939, or to the Urania, which showed cultural films. We no longer ventured into either theater after the above decree. A lawyer with an office on Jungfernstieg, however modest, might easily have been spotted.

One day our hankering for the "dream factory"—for ninety minutes' worth of something else to think about—became too much for us. (Young critics of old movies would find it easy to poke fun at our escapist dreams!) We headed for a poky little suburban movie house in Barmbek and asked for two good seats, because you could get a really stiff neck from sitting up front. All the good seats were taken, so we had to make the best of it. All of a sudden the usherette shone her flashlight over the first few rows and beckoned to us.

My heart stood still, my legs started trembling. Would we find ourselves confronted by two men in leather overcoats or brown or black uniforms? Had my father been recognized by someone?

"I have a box free now," the usherette said obligingly. She wasn't to know what she'd done. You couldn't have called us relieved—that would be far too mild a description—but going to the movies lost its appeal from then on.

Little Inge and I loved dancing. She was seventeen, I only sixteen, and in those days, when the age of majority was twenty-one, we had to get our parents' permission first. My mother rarely consented to chaperone us to a tea dance. Aside from the fact that we had no money to spare for tickets or dance dresses, she had other worries.

"Then for heaven's sake let us go on our own," we pleaded. "After all, we have to act grown-up enough in other respects." We enlisted the support of our fathers, who sadly backed us up. They appreciated how very far from carefree we were for our age. Carefree? By now, no dancing school, tennis club, or athletics club would accept us.

So we proudly set off, that summer afternoon in 1938, for the Orchideenkaffee near Dammtor station, once the site of a small zoo that my father and I had often visited on our Sunday walks together. I had saved up to buy myself a dark blue blouse of watered taffeta—the latest thing. It went against the grain to wear it with the skirt of my gray working suit, but I couldn't afford anything more suitable. The sun shone, the dance floor gleamed, and Laszlo Kurucz and his band struck us as "terrific."

When our rhythmical cavortings were interrupted by a Haydn minuet, we were joined at our table by my partner, Hans T. Little Inge and I had developed the knack of conjuring magical experiences out of very modest pleasures. To most people this would have been a run-of-the-mill tea dance—an experience to be repeated whenever they felt inclined; to us it was a whole succession of magical moments. That evening I called my parents and asked permission to stay out a bit longer. Hans was not only grown-up but "very respectable," I assured them, and he wanted to take me to "Tante Clara's." This was a popular cellar bar owned by a wine merchant named Benthin, whose plump and cheerful wife, Tante Clara, supplied the musical entertainment. Seated on stools around the upturned barrels that served as tables, customers listened raptly as she leveled a long pointer at a sheet of painted canvas and celebrated the funny pictures on it in song, accompanied by an accordion. Everyone joined in the choruses. Above us, swaying in a blue haze of tobacco smoke from countless pipes, dangled dried or imitation fish and carved wooden ships of all shapes and sizes. To the sixteen-year-old from Harvestehude, it was a unique and unforgettable occasion.

Hans, who was exactly twice my age, delivered a carefully worded speech while walking me home: a man of his mature years could very quickly tell whether two people were compatible, he was old enough to marry and keen to do so, and we must definitely get to know each other better.

I felt like Cinderella when the clock struck twelve. "I'm a leper," I told him. He thought I was drunk until I explained what a "first degree half-breed" was.

Principiis obsta! We resolved not to see each other again. It was a bad moment—my worst to date.

Then, one afternoon while I was still working for the patent attorney, Hans called me at the office. "I had a business appointment with the Gestapo at city hall," he said. He was an interior designer. "I inquired about our chances of obtaining a marriage permit. It can be done, you told me so yourself." I was almost speechless. "For God's sake," I said, "only on paper. Don't go giving those madmen ideas, or they'll watch us like hawks." Hans was unimpressed. "Not them," he said. "Friendly dissuasion, that's all they gave me." But I persisted. "It's impossible," I told him. "You'd risk losing your municipal contracts." The municipal contracts were a family tradition that dated back to his father's time.

Hans risked a lot more than that. One day, almost a year after our first and hitherto only meeting, we bumped into each other on the street. "There's no such thing as coincidence," he said, "only fate." And he bore me off to a dance hall on the corner of Lehmweg and Eppendorfer Weg. There was a little red light over the door. Innocuous though the place was, my parents wouldn't have approved—not that it took much to arouse parental misgivings in those days. Its name was the Half Moon.

We didn't talk about ourselves, just danced. Hans walked me home with a moon—a real one—hovering overhead. "We'll stick together," he said, "sink or swim." I was seventeen. Our daughter Barbara was born two and a half years later, by which time Hans was in the army.

In June 1938 Little Inge and I were christened by Pastor Walter Schmidt of Bremen, the husband of my mother's closest girlhood friend—a precautionary step of which he thoroughly approved. At least on paper—and at first glance—we no longer floated in a dangerous, conspicuous vacuum, though our baptismal certificates naturally made no difference to the "reprehensible" mixture of blood that flowed in our veins.

In November 1938 I traveled to Berlin to stay with my friend Manon and the new man in her life, a photographer named Umbo. I also saw my Aunt Alice, who was working as a nurse in a Jewish old people's home. She had invited me to dine with her at a restaurant on the night of November 10, because conditions at the home were deplorable, and I found the place so unutterably depressing that I wouldn't have eaten a bite. Once well-to-do but now stripped of their possessions and evicted from their houses and apartments, the poor old inmates waited with almost apathetic resignation—for what, they had no clear idea. . . .

There was a sudden commotion in the restaurant entrance, and some uniformed Nazis came tramping into the hushed, peaceful dining room. Their appearance instantly and irrevocably transformed our outlook on life. It was my very first sight of evil in action. The "non-Aryan" diners were hustled outside, so shocked and startled that none of them uttered a sound. Nothing could be heard but their receding footsteps, and I saw only one woman burst into tears.

My aunt remained quite calm. One of the uniformed figures marched up to our table. "I'm crippled in one leg, and my Christian niece accompanied me here." The only response was a barked request: "Papers!" With trembling fingers, I groped in my purse for my identity card. "So you aren't a Jewess?" I swallowed hard. "I live with my mother—she's the Aryan half of a privileged mixed marriage." How fluently the idiotic Nazi jargon came tripping off my tongue! The Brownshirt turned to my aunt. "And you're a nurse in an old folks' home?" Our papers were returned and the invaders left.

"I probably owe you my freedom," said Aunt Alice, "—for now." The truck that had been parked outside drove off at once. I couldn't face any more food, but Aunt Alice, ever practical, urged me to eat up. "You mustn't lose your appetite over a thing like that," she said. "This is only the start."

Too overwrought to sleep, Manon and I talked the rest of the night away. Being a half-Jewish divorcée, Manon couldn't legally marry her "Aryan" boyfriend, but she planned to go through a form of marriage on some little Baltic island where it mightn't occur to the local mayor to ask for her "Aryan credentials." She didn't succeed, incidentally, unlike another friend of mine, Ingrid L. Although such marriages were invalid, the neighbors weren't to know, so they regarded Ingrid's little son Kai as legitimate—a more important consideration then than it is now. The baby's stalwart "Aryan" father, a well-paid whaler, was away at sea and thus out of sight of the guardians of the law. They forgot him until war broke out, but he was later killed in action.

I caught a train back to Hamburg the next morning. The hours that preceded my departure were destined to go down in history as Kristallnacht, the "Night of Broken Glass." Just how "spontaneous" this eruption of "popular fury" was—the Nazis used these expressions ad nauseam—can be gauged from the phenomenal speed with which the following decrees were issued:

11.12.38:   Executive Order Pertaining to the Restoration of the Appearance of Streets in Respect of Jewish Business Premises

   1. All damage sustained by Jewish business premises and

homes in consequence of public indignation at interna-
tional Jewry's campaign against National Socialist Ger-
many will at once be made good by Jewish householders
and tradespeople.

2. The cost of repairs will be borne by the owners of the
Jewish businesses and residences affected. All insurance
claims lodged by Jews of German nationality will be
sequestered for the benefit of the State. (P. 254)

On November 9, the third secretary of the German embassy in Paris, Ernst Eduard vom Rath, had been assassinated by a German Jewish refugee named Herschel Grynspan. Strangely enough, our authorities must have had prior knowledge of this incident.

This murder heralded the darkest period in our country's history, becoming a justification for all that ensued—all that might have been foreseen by any reader of Hitler's *Mein Kampf*: it ultimately led to the Final Solution.

Every decree issued between then and 1945 was one more nail in the coffin of human dignity and human life itself. To quote Robert Kempner's introduction to *Das Sonderrecht für die Juden im NS-Staat*:

"They were deprived of their occupations, robbed of their property, forbidden to inherit or bequeath, forbidden to sit on park benches or keep canaries, forbidden to use public transportation [Author's note: except to a very limited degree], forbidden to frequent restaurants, concerts, theaters, and movie houses. They were subject to specific racial laws, stripped of all their civil rights, denied freedom of movement. Their human rights and human dignity were trampled in the dust until they were deported to concentration camps and consigned to the gas chambers."

This process, with all its atrocious concomitants, began on November 10, 1938.

11.10.38: *Further to tonight's directive from CdSiPo [chief of Security Police], I advise you that Dachau, Buchenwald, and Sachsenhausen [Oranienburg] concentration camps are each in a position to accommodate ten thousand detainees. (P. 253)*

11.10.38: *Jews found with arms in their possession are to be held in custody for twenty years. (P. 253)*

November 11 was my brother's birthday. We had laid the table and lit fifteen candles, but we waited in vain for my father to turn up. He had been ordered off a streetcar and taken to Oranienburg-Sachsenhausen concentration camp, near Berlin.

I recorded my impressions of his homecoming in December 1938. The magazine *Umschau* published them in 1947—my very first appearance in print. Everything was still so fresh in my mind that I found it hard to take a detached view of what had happened.

One day we received a card with a red border. "Sender: Detainee Felix Hecht. Detainee's No. . . . ." Then: "Oranienburg Concentration Camp, near Berlin." He was released shortly before Christmas.

12.12.38: *All Jewish detainees over the age of fifty are to be released. Discharged prisoners must report to the police at once. (P. 266)*

He turned up with a shaven skull, bent and gaunt, a weary man with weary eyes. And he was so cold, so very cold. The cold had stored itself in his limbs while he was breaking stones in the teeth of the icy November wind. Camp regulations prescribed light clothing only, and anyone who secreted newspaper under his shirt for warmth was beaten half to death. It had been intimated to my father and all the others released that day in December 1938 that anyone who spoke of his detention outside would be in serious trouble. We *wanted* him to speak, though. Our discretion went without saying, and anyway, he had to tell someone. In a low voice punctuated by the hollow cough that lingered with him for a long time to come, he recounted his terrible experiences. If he hadn't been our own father, a qualified lawyer, and in his right mind, we would never have believed him.

But we had to resume our daily lives and be our normal selves without even hinting at what we had heard. The Todtmanns were the only people I dared confide in. Frau Todtmann gave me a big package of groceries for my father and told me, with absolute sincerity, "The Führer knows nothing of this."

We "half-breeds" were slowly becoming inured to fear. "Aryan" friends would sometimes invite us to share their relatively carefree existence. We were fortunate in having these opportunities to enjoy ourselves in cheerful company, unlike our Jewish friends and relations, but we also had to live with the awareness of being better off than they were. The real sufferers didn't begrudge us our fun, but we weren't always as generous to ourselves.

During the summer of 1938, a London dance craze had crossed the channel and caught on at the Café Vaterland, where patrons were taught the steps at teatime on the little circular dance floor. The "Lambeth Walk" was an innocently amusing novelty dance with a catchy tune. One afternoon Hans and I whiled away an hour or two prancing around and clapping our hands obediently in time to the music.

Then came the inevitable letdown. "Who knows," I said as we were walking home, "that may be one of our pleasantest memories ever." It was a prescient remark.

Being English, the "Lambeth Walk" was of course banned when war broke out. When I first heard it again in 1980, the memories it revived were bittersweet.

THE FIRST YEAR
OF THE WAR
(1 9 3 9)

10.17.39:   *If Jews and persons of German blood occupy the*
same building, and if the Germans [sic!] *consti-*
tute the majority of the occupants of that build-
ing, the Jews will not take part in air raid practices.
If the contrary applies, Jews will carry out prac-
tices on their own. *(P. 306)*

PRIOR TO THE INTRODUCTION of the yellow star which every Jew had to wear, someone had come up with another bright idea:

8.17.38: *From 1.1.39 Jews who do not bear one of the forenames listed as a Jewish forename in the Interior Ministry circular dated 8.18.38 must assume the name "Israel" (for male persons) or "Sara" (for female persons). (P. 237)*

Because my father's first name was Felix—the Happy One!—and not Isaak, Isidor, or Mosche, he, too, received a new birth certificate from Registry Office 3a, Kolonnaden 3, Hamburg. It bore the following note: "The aforesaid child has assumed the additional name 'Israel.' "

It was as simple as that. From now on, anyone who asked to see your identity card could tell your racial origins at a glance. By the time passports were stamped with a "J," as they very soon were, no person of the Jewish faith could travel abroad unrecognized for what he was.

On January 28, 1939, my father received a letter from the Gestapo revoking his permission to appear before the Hamburg courts.

9.27.38:   Executive Order Pertaining to the Reich Citizenship Law

> *The profession of attorney is closed to Jews. Any Jews still practicing as attorneys will quit the bar by 11.30.38 (or, in certain cases, somewhat later). The judicatory will permit Jewish legal consultants to advise and represent Jews. Veterans among the retiring attorneys may, if in need, be granted revocable subsistence allowances payable out of the incomes of Jewish legal consultants. The latter will retain a proportion of their fees as remuneration. (P. 242)*

There being no well-to-do Jewish clients left, my father's income had dried up. He was therefore entitled to claim a subsistence allowance under the 1938 decree, though this was a laborious and demeaning business. I came across a letter from the Bar Association in Berlin, dated November 1941, which allotted my father RM 170 a month but warned him to expect further cuts in the future. It additionally pointed out that he qualified for a grant only because he had two underage children.

Like many communications from attorneys who had taken over the clients and, thus, the incomes of their Jewish colleagues, this letter conveyed not a shadow of regret, not a hint of shame. Its tone was chilly.

My wages as an office worker just about covered our monthly gas bill, once I had deducted an agreed share for myself, so we drew a supplementary allowance from the public welfare office—not in those days a legal entitlement. In return for this meager financial support, lucky though we were to get it at all, my mother had to work in a frightful sewing room a long way from home. She also earned some extra money by cleaning house for a doctor's wife in the neighborhood. This lady, who was a Tartar in other respects, overlooked her lack of dexterity with a bucket and scrubbing brush and her inability to polish tiles and parquet floors. At least she was one of those who secretly deplored our lot.

One evening our lodger Ali took me to Schwanenwiek to see a friend named Hans Wolffheim, whom we found ensconced amid piles of books in a little garret overlooking the Alster.

Ali introduced us. "Aside from being as much of a mongrel as you are," he told me, "Hans has more brains than anyone I know." He turned to Wolffheim. "Tell her your specialties, Hans."

Wolffheim, who was another "first degree half-breed," shrugged and smiled. "Philosophy, German, English—oh yes, and psychology, worse luck."

"And now," said Ali, "he sits here vegetating."

"Surely not," I said, surveying all the books. Hans Wolffheim had taken a degree in 1933, just in time, but the Nuremberg Laws disqualified him from joining the university faculty. Restricted to "employment of a subordinate nature," he spent his days working in a textile factory. It was 1946 before he obtained a lectureship, though he was subsequently appointed to the chair of modern German literature at Hamburg.

Wolffheim derived a certain pleasure from my interest in literature. He used to read aloud to us for hours on end, notably from such authors as Thomas Mann, in exile since 1933, and Karl Wolfskehl, who had lived in Italy until 1938 and fled from the Fascists to New Zealand. (Wolffheim later founded a study center for expatriate German literature at Hamburg

University.) A friend of ours from now on, he occasionally rustled up some genuine Indian tea, which was getting steadily scarcer. To me, tea was not only conversationally stimulating but something akin to an elixir of life.

For victims of Nazi oppression, the outbreak of war on September 1, 1939, spelled emotional conflicts of unimaginable intensity. Nazi Germany's enemies were, after all, our potential liberators. Every bomb that fell brought liberation nearer, but it also fell on us, our friends and neighbors—on the people to whom we had belonged till 1933.

In 1946, when I called on the chief rabbi of the Jewish community in Freiburg, who had recently returned from Theresienstadt, in the hope of learning something about my father's fate, he asked when I had last been in Hamburg. "Not since the terror raids of July 1943," I told him. Goebbels's term for Allied air attacks came quite naturally to me—it had passed into our vocabulary, too—but the old man nearly exploded. In his view, no response to German acts of aggression could be termed a "terror raid."

> 9.1.39: *By order of local police authorities, Jews are prohibited from walking the streets (being outside their homes) after 8 P.M. (9 P.M. in summer). (P. 303)*

Even my "privileged" father had to observe this rule as far as possible. We had long ago ceased to speculate on the reasons for such edicts. Foreigners must have found them less intelligible, however, because on September 15, 1939, a "confidential directive" was issued to the German press:

> 9.15.39 *Foreign newspapers have stated that Jews in Germany are no longer permitted to walk the streets after 8 P.M. This*

is correct. All local authorities in the Reich have issued an order to that effect, on the ground that Jews have not infrequently taken advantage of the blackout to molest Aryan women. (P. 305)

9.20.39: *Jews of German nationality and stateless Jews are forbidden to own radio receivers. This prohibition covers Aryans living on Jewish premises, and also half-breeds. Special regulations apply to mixed marriages. (P. 305)*

Because we lived with our "Aryan" mother, we could turn on the radio as often as we liked. Whenever we listened to music, to a concert or a lecture, it heightened our sense of guilt at being better off than our neighbors.

"RACIAL DISGRACE"
AND PLANS TO EMIGRATE
(1940)

9.18.35: *Persons implicated in cases of racial disgrace are to be taken into custody. (P. 131)*

9.26.35: *Where instances of "racially disgraceful conduct" antedate the promulgation of the new Jewish laws, authorities are recommended to refrain from drastic measures except in particularly flagrant cases of seduction or rape.*

Those committing offenses subsequent to the promulgation of the new Jewish laws will be ruthlessly prosecuted. (P. 132)

WHEN WILL IT BE our turn? The thought that had haunted our lives like a waking nightmare became reality, as it had for so many others, a few weeks before Easter 1940. Here is how I described it to the Hamburg Reparations Office in September 1961, in support of a (rejected) claim for compensation:

"Some weeks before Easter, my mother was arrested for allegedly committing an act of 'racial disgrace' with her divorced husband, my father, and taken to city hall. My father, who had lived with us for five years after the divorce and paid us regular visits thereafter, was also arrested.

"Late the same evening, my mother came home. She fainted on entering the apartment, and we put her to bed. When she recovered consciousness, she enlisted the advice of our lodger Ali. Apparently, she had been threatened and bullied, under extremely undignified circumstances, into admitting an act of 'racial disgrace.' She now wished to retract this admission at once, in writing. An attorney, Dr. Harms, called on us and took her retraction down. The Gestapo's response was to summon my mother again by telephone, though she was really in no fit state to leave her bed. 'Detainee Sillich'—as she had to call herself when reporting her presence, standing at attention in her cell—was not reunited with us until the Thursday before Easter, three weeks later. My father was released the same day. I myself paid one visit to city hall through the good offices of Dr. Harms. Though treated in an exceedingly sarcastic manner, I was informed that I could deliver some articles of clothing to the Hamburg-Fuhlsbüttel detention center. After her release, my mother told us that she had had to sign a written undertaking never to see my father again, and that she was to be held responsible for ensuring that my brother and I formed no relationships with 'Aryan' partners. Otherwise, she would at once be rearrested.

"We do not know whether such statements were to be taken seriously. What is certain is that from then until April 23, 1945, the date of our liberation in Staufen/Breisgau, my mother never shook off her terrible fears and has since required constant medical attention."

This factual account cannot convey our state of mind during those weeks. But for our friend Ali and the attorney, who made unremitting efforts to secure our parents' release, the suspense would have been almost unbearable, because no word of their fate was allowed to filter through to us.

I began by describing the world in which my mother grew up. During her three weeks in custody—over which I prefer to draw a veil—she began to feel as if her childhood were only a dream. The two worlds seemed so utterly incompatible.

"That first day," she said, "I met the kind of girls I'd never come up against before. . . ."

"Whores, you mean?"

She was relieved that I'd absolved her from saying the word. It had never passed her lips before, any more than the girls themselves had formed part of her social environment.

"They were old hands, you see. They couldn't have been

nicer—they teased me a little for being so frightened and impractical, but they weren't in there for political reasons and had no conception of what it meant. They rolled me some cigarettes—out of butts, imagine!" We couldn't repress a wry laugh at this, but she went on, "You'd never believe how quickly a person can grow to appreciate anything that seems like a humane gesture in inhuman surroundings. . . ."

But what had actually led up to her imprisonment?

April 1942: *Jews are forbidden to visit the homes of Aryans and persons living in mixed matrimony. (P. 369)*

This regulation was observed long before it appeared in writing, but who would have dreamed that the Nuremberg Laws could apply to a divorced couple who had produced two "offspring"? Well, now we knew.

The layout of our Hansastrasse apartment proved disastrous. Originally one floor of a spacious town house, it had later been divided into two suites of rooms separated by a communicating door, which could be locked. Anyone wanting to pay us a visit in the rear suite had to pass through the suite at the front. The latter was rented by a small, private old people's home, and it was those ladies, Party members one and all, who had denounced my parents.

We continued to live cheek by jowl with them—we had no choice—but my father had to shun their "Aryan" orbit from then on, and was consequently banished from the family table.

The former Fräulein von Sillich, who had once been privileged to receive a letter of condolence from the duke of Meiningen on the sudden death of her father (she reverently preserved it in a casket) and had seen that same father buried with full military honors—whose upbringing, in short, had been founded on the traditional values of the imperial era—had now become acquainted with certain previously unimagined and unimaginable things: for example, the inside of a jail. Much the same could be said of Felix Hecht, erstwhile sergeant of the Seventh (Seydlitz) Cuirassiers, a regiment of heavy cavalry based at Halberstadt. For all his experience of life and knowledge of the world, he had found it impossible to conceive—until *Kristallnacht*—that his active service in the First World War, which earned him the Iron Cross Second Class (Jewish soldiers were seldom awarded any higher decoration), would fail to protect him from the gathering storm.

One day in the summer of 1940 I was summoned to report for a medical examination. All German girls not undergoing higher education or vocational training were obliged to do a year's national service, usually as farmhands or domestic help for mothers of large families. "Oh God," I groaned to Hans Wolffheim, "that's all I needed!" After the treatment we'd received from them, did the authorities really expect us to perform this "honorary service" for the German nation?

Wolffheim came around the same evening, bearing a packet of tea. "Drink some just before your medical," he advised, faintly amused at the idea of a townee like me wielding a pick and shovel. "We're so unused to the stuff these days, it's bound to give you palpitations."

So I drank plenty—I've seldom enjoyed the delicious beverage less—and reported to the medical center. It was crowded with "Aryan" girls. Most of them seemed in high spirits, and anyone who may secretly have been unenthusiastic took care not to show it. The doctor treated me sympathetically, in a detached sort of way, because I saw no reason to conceal my "half-breed" status and circumstances. Although he might have drafted me on principle, he didn't. He returned my employment record stamped "Compulsory One-Year Service Deferred." My deferment ran for only twelve months, but by 1941 the authorities had largely stopped bothering about the likes of us.

Incidental note: I needn't have drunk all that tea—I'd have had palpitations anyway.

[1935:] Re Art and Antique Dealers

> *Pursuant to paragraph 10 of Decree No. 1 pertaining to the implementation of the Reich Chamber of Culture Law of 11.1.33, I refuse you admission to the Reich Chamber of Fine Arts and debar you from continuing to pursue the occupation of art and antique dealer. I grant you four weeks' grace in which to reorganize or liquidate your business.* (P. 149)

Uncle Edgar, who had taken over the Rembrandthaus, my grandfather's old and reputable business in the Colonnades, was also affected by a decree of this nature. Although trade had dwindled badly, we were much attached to the remains of this onetime family institution. Now it was to be "reorganized," in this case meaning sold. The purchaser, I believe, was the firm's former janitor.

Most of my father's fellow attorneys had emigrated, and his only partner had committed suicide. How could he emigrate, though, without a vestige of capital, without us children, and, last but not least, with no hope of reestablishing his practice in some foreign land? He was too old to go to Palestine as a pioneer. Doctors could make a fresh start abroad without too much difficulty, whereas lawyers had no such professional prospects. Honduras and Shanghai were potential places of

75

refuge for impecunious Jews, though certain restrictions applied there, too.

"What on earth could I do in a Chinese city?" my father protested, and he had a point. What *could* a Hamburg attorney have done in the Far East, in a city that had been occupied by Japan, an Axis power, since its seizure from the Chinese in 1937?

My relatives from Hagedornstrasse, Uncle Edgar, Aunt Hanna, and cousin Hans, booked passage to Shanghai in 1940. They offered to send written confirmation, on arrival, that they would house me if I chose to join them there. I could then get some kind of job and try to arrange a passage for my father as well.

I agreed, though without any clear idea of what I was doing. Perhaps I saw it as my father's last chance of escape, but what of my unfortunate mother? She had already lost her health and her faith in human nature. Was she now to lose her family into the bargain?

"You'll still have Wolfgang," I consoled her, "and we'll probably be able to come back sometime."

For the present, however, Hitler's armies remained victorious.

It all went very quickly. Jews were confined to their homes after dark and the train didn't leave the central station until midnight, so it was late afternoon when the Hechts made their way to the Hotel Reichshof to while away their last night in Germany. Because of the curfew, only Little Inge and I could accompany them.

The emigrants were depressed, dispirited, and filled with premature homesickness. Our family had, after all, lived on the banks of the Elbe for two generations. Besides, we all

dreaded that some terrible hitch might occur at the last moment, because it went without saying that the permits and
papers had to be examined yet again by some official of for-
bidding mien. All in all, it was a lugubrious occasion.

When the time came, we escorted the trio across the dark-
ened street to the gloomy station entrance. "Please don't come
onto the platform with us," said Aunt Hanna, then: "Happy
landings in Shanghai!" (When they got there, any exultation
the new arrivals felt was dampened by the sight of a swastika
flag flying from the masthead of a German ship berthed alongside the Huangpu waterfront!)

In February 1982 I was reminded of my Aunt Hanna's de-
scriptions of life in Shanghai by a West German radio recon-
struction of this largely unknown form of emigration.

The Oriental mentality forbade "whites," or Europeans in
general, to perform "menial" tasks. German Jews elsewhere
in the world had long ago abandoned such class-conscious
notions, many of them having gone into domestic service in
Britain and the United States. In Shanghai, however, Euro-
pean and American residents impressed on all newcomers that
these unwritten rules must be observed. A local Jewish Welfare
Association saw to it that emigrants were housed and com-
munally fed, but they found their enforced idleness hard to
bear. Only the craftsmen among them, most of whom came
from Eastern Europe, managed to set up small workshops and
escape from the slums. This came to a stop in May 1943, when
all stateless persons, including Jewish immigrants, were herded
together and confined in a ghetto. The craftsmen, too, were
forced to abandon the fruits of their hard work and move to
the ghetto, a slum quarter infested with typhus and cholera.
Many of the inmates died.

I was naturally unaware of this when the promised letter arrived and I began making arrangements to leave for Shanghai. While my poor mother suffered in courageous silence (as befitted an officer's daughter) and my father bottled up his sense of guilt, I myself succumbed to a thrill of anticipation and adventure. After all, I was still technically a child.

Our last objets d'art were sold, and the balance of my fare was given me by a friend of the family, the writer William Quindt, who lived in Blankenese. A well-traveled man with a wide knowledge of people and places at home and abroad— he had been press agent for the Sarrasani Circus for years— Herr Quindt not only detested the Nazis to the point of nausea but helped us on numerous occasions. I presented my papers, obtained a travel permit, and bought my Trans-Siberian Railroad ticket. To a twenty-year-old in the days when foreign travel was neither as commonplace nor as relatively inexpensive as it is today, nothing could have seemed more glamorously exotic, especially in wartime.

I felt quite odd when my fingers finally closed on the sheaf of tickets that would take me all the way across the Soviet Union to China. When the odd sensation persisted and I started feeling actively sick, I went to the doctor. "You're going to have a baby," he told me.

I handed back my tickets and wrote to Shanghai. My dear, good mother now had occasion to discover that even an illegitimate grandchild—a phenomenon alien to her world of ideas— deserved to be hailed with joy if it banished her misgivings about a daughter's departure for the Far East.

And my father's prospects of emigrating? "Never mind," he said, "I'm delighted about the baby." For a while he was alone in his delight. I was filled with foreboding.

My cousin Jack Hecht, now a resident of Alamo, California, tape-recorded his recollections for me in September 1982:

"We left Hamburg in 1940, when I was eight years old. From Hamburg we traveled by train via Berlin to Danzig, then on by air to Moscow, where we boarded the Trans-Siberian Express. We traveled across the USSR for a whole week, through Siberia to Vladivostok, then to Harbin in Manchukuo and on to Dairen. It was awfully cold, I remember, and I couldn't understand why we had to go so far from home. From Dairen we sailed down the Chinese coast in a little steamer, sleeping in the hold with some Japanese soldiers. We reached Shanghai two days later.

"We were greeted by the Jewish community, and my father managed to rent us a room—we referred to it as a small apartment—in the French concession. In those days Shanghai was an international settlement under Japanese control and British, French, and American supervision. In our quarter the street names were French, as were the police and the military. My father, who had three hundred dollars on deposit at a Japanese bank, used the money to open a small art dealer's shop. The local inhabitants were very interested in objets d'art. We had divided up the premises, and we ate and slept there, too. The foreign troops withdrew when war broke out between Japan and America after the attack on Pearl Harbor, and the Japanese occupied the entire city without firing a shot. That was in December 1941.

"In May 1943 the Japanese decreed that all stateless persons not in possession of passports should move to Hongkiu, a ghetto area. This decree principally affected the Jewish immigrants, who now, like my father, lost their modest livelihoods all over again. Father was assigned one room, and we had to share the kitchen and bathroom with six other families.

No interest in art could survive under such circumstances, and our minor material advantages came to an end.

"I went to the Jewish community school, where German teachers taught us the usual subjects. We boys played football and the grown-ups founded sports clubs, so life went on like that all through the war. American bombers sometimes raided Japanese military installations in the city.

"Then came July 17, 1945. It was a very cloudy day. I and a lot of other children were playing outside the house where we lived. We could hear airplanes but not see them, the clouds were so thick. They came nearer, and when I looked up at the sky I saw little black specks of dust raining down on us. They were bombs. One of them exploded in front of our house. I ran into the kitchen. The entrance was behind the house. Everything was littered with glass, and the plaster was flaking off the walls. My father came toward me, bleeding from a big wound over his heart. He was still on his feet. I shouted, 'Papa, you're wounded!' Then he collapsed. A piece of shrapnel must have sailed through the open window and hit him. My mother was unhurt. She'd been in the kitchen, my father in the living room.

"I still believe that something could have been done for my father if so many people around us hadn't been injured at the same time. He bled to death. The doctors couldn't be everywhere at once.

"The war ended in August 1945, and the Jewish community of America sent us money, food, and clothing. There were eighteen thousand of us by that time, all immigrants from Germany, Austria, Poland, and Hungary."

That was how my nice, jovial Uncle Edgar met his end. Although Aunt Hanna never got over his death, she was a very courageous woman. She trained to become a nurse and worked at a Shanghai hospital until she and cousin Hans were offered a chance to emigrate to San Francisco in the summer of 1949.

I've often wondered where *I* would have been during that air raid, in the kitchen or the living room. . . .

I tried to find out how the Jews of Shanghai were treated by the Nazi Party's local representatives. A diplomat who was stationed there at the time told me that the Japanese didn't give "a damn" about the Nazis' anti-Jewish campaign. They simply confined all stateless persons in Hongkiu.

The Japanese who acted as "boss" of the ghetto, a man named Goya, was interned by the Americans. According to cousin Hans, they later released him because he had refused to do what the Nazis allegedly asked him to do: build some gas chambers.

THE LONG YEAR
(1941)

9.1.41: *With effect from 9.15.41, Jews who have attained the age of seven are forbidden to show themselves in public without a Jewish star. Jews are forbidden to leave their residential area without written police permission, and to wear decorations or other medals.*

This does not apply to Jewish husbands living in mixed matrimony if there exist offspring of their marriages who do not count as Jews, or if their only son has been killed in action, nor to Jewish wives of childless mixed marriages for the duration of such marriages. (P. 347)

As SOON AS I KNEW I was pregnant, I wrote to Hans. Although it was a hazardous and impractical course of action, he spoke to his sergeant, the first person in authority to approach when applying for permission to marry (which was sometimes granted, so it was said, though never to my knowledge). The outcome was disastrous, of course. When Barbara was born he wrote me from the Russian front that he hoped he would never come back. That wasn't a very cheering letter for a young mother to receive during her confinement, but I'd grown accustomed to expecting nothing, not even consolation. Hans had gone through a great deal by that time, partly on my account and partly because of his appalling experiences at the front.

His wish was fulfilled. He paid one visit to Hamburg and made his little daughter's acquaintance, but was killed in action at Lepel on June 29, 1944.

I needed a maternity dress and was allocated some extra clothing coupons. My mother and I set off on a shopping expedition. While we were walking down Grindelallee, something unforgettable happened.

Father was coming toward us on the other side of the street. We caught sight of each other at the same instant. Mother turned deathly pale and stopped short. Father, too, paused for a moment. "For God's sake keep moving," I said. "Someone may be spying on us—they may think we arranged it." Mother walked on. Father walked on. Mother started crying.

"Shall we buy the silly dress another time?" I asked.

"No," she said, "that wouldn't help either." Then she said, "If I'd known all this, I'd never have divorced him. If anything happens to him, I'll always feel I'm to blame."

She nursed that belief till the day she died in 1979. It was a long time.

My father had been compelled to move out when the Edgar Hechts left for Shanghai. He now lived in one small room in Dillstrasse, which had gradually become a kind of ghetto. That room, with its bed, bookcase, hot plate, and cluttered chairs, still haunts my dreams. . . .

My father liked to keep a miniature reference library of newspaper articles on subjects of particular interest to him. That had presented few problems in a house or apartment, but in one diminutive room? He needed an occupation that would take his mind off things, now more than ever, so the walls were lined with ever-growing mountains of newsprint.

Did we devote enough attention to him at this time? Why didn't we go and help him sort out his stacks of newspapers? Why didn't we cook for him? I still have his cookbook, the flyleaf of which bears a note of the pages to be consulted when braising steak and cooking rice. He was fifty-seven years old and a stranger to the inside of a kitchen when he started experimenting with a hot plate.

Why trouble to record such details? Because they form

part of the mosaic. One's conscience can be pricked by the strangest little things. . . .

My father was exempted from wearing a star. So, of course, was my mother, and the same applied to Wolfgang and me. Little Inge's position was different because her mother had converted to Judaism on her marriage, so the children of that marriage were *Geltungsjuden*, a Nazi neologism implying that they were technically and formally Jewish. By a very rare stroke of good fortune, Little Inge's status remained temporarily undetected. Besides, we had both been baptized in 1938. Although this wouldn't have helped in a real emergency, there were occasions when officials refrained from insisting on documentary proof of one's "Aryan" ancestry. Little Inge's father did have to wear the star, however, because he had divorced her mother at her own request and married a Jewess.

Our relations and many of our friends were obliged to wear what the Nazis regarded as a badge of shame, which had by law to be prominently displayed. When "star wearers" paid us a visit, they would try to obscure or conceal the yellow emblem because all such visits were prohibited. We had good reason to fear the Nazi crones in the front apartment, but we also feared for ourselves. We feared that someday, if an explosive situation arose, we ourselves would avert our eyes, say nothing, walk on—that we ourselves would be found wanting in what was termed backbone.

3.29.41: *The Reich Association [of Jews] has until April 1, 1941, to supply the RSHA [Central State Security Bureau] with a full list of all Jewish apartments in Aryan buildings. This list must include addresses, number of rooms, and additional details. (P. 338)*

There was an acceleration and accumulation of horrors in 1941. The first trainloads of deportees left for the East, and decrees were issued with the ultimate aim of "expelling" the Jews. These ranged from the registration of their living quarters and all their possessions to the following, logical, edict:

11.15.42: *Jews may no longer keep household pets. (P. 364)*

I say logical, because the authors of the Final Solution wished to spare themselves the necessity of slaughtering abandoned pets as well as their owners.

Jews were also subject to increasingly ominous cuts in their food rations. Unless they received covert help—and many tradespeople were secretly charitable to their long-established Jewish customers—they wasted away for all to see (not that their plight hadn't been universally obvious ever since the wearing of yellow stars was made compulsory).

Then came another turn of the screw:

4.20.41: *Foodstuffs received by Jews in packages from abroad are to be deducted from their food rations. (P. 339)*

All else apart, Jews had been treated as enemies since the outbreak of war, and their German nationality had been revoked.

For all that, "first degree half-breeds" like us had many aids to distraction, notably the movies. When I saw a 1982 revival of *Quax der Bruchpilot*, a Heinz Rühmann comedy made in 1941, my mind went back to the wartime evening when Little Inge and I had reveled in its innocent humor. Rühmann had poked fun at the concept of iron discipline with admirable understatement, though without actually demolishing it. Germany was fighting a war, after all, even if it wasn't his war or ours. (We only found out later that he was one of the many stars whose marriages to or relationships with "non-Aryans" put them at Goebbels's mercy, so they couldn't have been half as cheerful as they had to make out!) Thank you anyway, Heinz Rühmann, for giving us so much enjoyment.

Not wanting the evening to end as soon as the movie was over, we headed for a little wine bar in Grindelallee, close enough to home for us to get back in time if the air raid sirens sounded an early warning. Almost at once, we were joined at our table by two SS men. Little Inge, whose blonde hair was almost certainly to blame for this dubious honor, made a warning noise in her throat. "Aryan" girls could have afforded to get up and go; we couldn't.

Our companions were caricatures of their kind: glass eyes would have looked more human. I am adding nothing and leaving a good deal unsaid when I record that, during our conversation, one of them suddenly began to brag about his maltreatment of Jews in a concentration camp. Although many SS men would never have dreamed of raising the subject, I'm sure, this one really did. I don't recall how we managed to get away, but we never again visited the place unescorted.

We were sitting at the breakfast table on June 22, 1941, when Ali came rushing in. Pale to the roots of his hair, he told us that Hitler had declared war on Russia.

Ali once took me and Little Inge to the Bronzekeller, a cabaret on Carl Muck Platz where the artists had retained a lot of political courage and performed from the heart. None of their numbers approximated to the type of entertainment favored by the Nazis, and they still used satirical material by Mascha Kaléko and Kurt Tucholsky.

At the Bronzekeller I got to know Otto Larsen, who had a big, well-lit studio near the Kleiner Jungfernstieg, with a view across the Alster. Very alert to the needs of the time, Otto manufactured decorative tiles. Articles suitable as presents were unobtainable, so he not only supplied them but convinced the citizens of Hamburg that their dearest wish was to own one of his ceramic coffee-pot stands or jardinieres. Once I had been taught how to mix and use china paints, I specialized in colorful fishing smacks with swelling sails and dainty Chinese maidens carrying parasols. We drew our motifs on greaseproof paper, pricked the outlines with a pin, laid the sheets down on tiles, sprinkled them with powdered granite—and there were the silhouettes of our boats and Chinese girls, transferred to the tiles and ready to be colored in. Waves could be imbued with movement by varying the pressure of one's brush. The work was enjoyable as well as remunerative, and some of the friendships I formed at the studio have endured to this day. It was there that I got to know Olli Cohnheim, who already owned the country retreat at Staufen where she put us up after the great air raid. I obtained a labor permit entitling me to pursue an occupation—though only in a "non-self-employed" capacity, of course—and when Otto Larsen was finally drafted and had to close the studio down, I continued to work on my own account. My customers among the storekeepers of Hamburg never asked to see my "Aryan credentials," and the local revenue office proved equally incurious.

7.19.40: *Jews are debarred from being telephone subscribers. Exceptions will be made for legal consultants, medical practitioners, and persons living in privileged mixed matrimony. (P. 325)*

My daughter Barbara was born on August 26, 1941. My father had wangled me into the Elisabeth Hospital, formerly a Masonic institution, and managed to get me a private room there. Anxious to avoid awkward questions, I paid the hospital fees out of my own earnings. I was very well treated in spite of my unmarried state. Nothing marred the tranquillity of my confinement except the early morning din from a neighboring slaughterhouse, which I found excruciating.

In those days, parents were issued lists of officially approved names. Children born in the Thousand Year Reich could not be given names from the Old Testament—Esther or Rachel, for instance. Much to our secret amusement, Maria was considered acceptable!

The delighted grandfather came to see me every morning, the youthful grandmother every afternoon. Caution dictated the strictest adherence to this schedule because we didn't know how closely their enforced separation was being supervised by Nazi informers, and Barbara's birth would have been an opportunity to catch them out.

My father adored taking the little "second degree half-breed" for walks, though the preliminaries this entailed were elaborate in the extreme. Being a "legal consultant" and exempt from wearing a star, he was at liberty to use public telephone booths, so he would dial our number and hang up without speaking. My mother then carried Barbara downstairs to the lobby—we lived on the third floor—where she had previously left the baby carriage. She made her way cautiously to the front door, and when my father came into view on the corner of Hansastrasse and Grindelallee, she would trundle Barbara outside, dart back into the house, and wait till the two of them were together. The baby's return followed the same pattern. We had long ago ceased to chafe at the indignity of such situations.

Although I received a child allowance from the German armed forces, the arrival of a new little family member made it necessary for me to earn some additional money. The ever-helpful Rolf Sommer had cleverly contrived to get his business in Kleine Bäckerstrasse classified as "essential to the war effort," so I continued to work there half-days. The evenings—and many, many nights in the air raid shelter—I devoted to painting tiles. By now I was adept at balancing a drawing board on my knee and working in the dimly lit cellar. Looking back, I don't know how I managed to keep a steady hand when air raids were in progress, but the dull detonations we heard were said to be our own antiaircraft guns, and our part of the city wasn't hit until the summer of 1943. Until then, we seem to have preserved a strange kind of fortitude or fatalism.

My friend Ingrid also led a very difficult existence in Hansastrasse, where she lived with her little son Kai and her Jewish mother. I taught her to paint tiles, and we jointly pursued this colorful activity for a couple of years. Ingrid moved south to the Fichtelgebirge after the big raid, but not before she had braved the turmoil that reigned in the blazing city and procured her mother some false papers. They both survived the war.

12.19.38:   *Permission for Jews and first degree half-breeds to change their names will as a rule be denied. (P. 269)*

One day in the summer of 1941, my mother received a visit from an official of some kind. Didn't my brother and I also wish to assume the name "von Sillich"? The decree of December 1938 must have escaped his notice. Wolfgang and I dismissed the suggestion, but I still wonder if we would have been quite so adamant if our surname had been typically Jewish.

I recall this incident in tribute to our friend Olli Cohnheim. Being only a "second degree half-breed," she might well have obtained permission to drop the name that had proved such a handicap, but she clung to it through thick and thin. Olli was compelled to close her Hamburg bookbindery because the "Cohnheim" frightened customers away. She ran a small handicrafts business for a while after moving to the Black Forest, but that eventually folded, too. When I myself moved south and mentioned her name to a prospective purchaser of my painted tiles, he told me that a Jewess's recommendation was no recommendation at all. In spite of everything, Olli never dropped her father's "suspect" name.

Incidental note: Germans of the younger generation are hardly aware that such a thing as a "typically Jewish" name exists.

10.24.41: *Persons of German blood who openly display their friendly relations with Jews are to be temporarily detained on educational grounds, or, in more serious cases, committed to a grade one concentration camp for a term of up to three months. The Jewish party will in every case be detained in a concentration camp until further notice. (P. 353)*

Wolfgang and I were not prepared to forgo our non-Jewish friends. As long as they had the guts, so did we. Although this seems a rather rash attitude in retrospect, we doubted the authorities could keep us under constant surveillance for years on end. Our parents lived in fear, but we had become inured to the idea that our life was a macabre dance on the edge of a volcano. Did we really have to spend every waking minute wondering when it would erupt?

Little Inge recalls:

"I was out walking with Rudi Samson, my friend from the 'Comrades.' We were strolling side by side down a narrow street to Rothenbaumchaussee—Turmweg, I think it was. Rudi was wheeling his bicycle. Two men in SS uniform came toward us from the direction of Reitplatz, and before we could dodge them one of them planted himself in front of Rudi and started brandishing his riding crop. 'You Jewish lout!' he said. 'This'll teach you to run around with a German girl!' Before he could lash out, the other one pulled him away. The 'German girl' was me.

"Rudi emigrated to Holland with his parents soon afterward and died in a concentration camp."

Ali had introduced Little Inge and me to some friends who used to go sailing on the Elbe from the yacht basin at Schulau, near Wedel. For us this marked the beginning of a pleasant interlude—our happiest in all those wartime years. Out on the Elbe we lost our dread of the ominous ring at the door before dawn, the Gestapo's favorite visiting time. Our new friends, who were all in more or less middle-class jobs, ranged from dentists and painters to technical draftsmen. United in their hatred of the Nazis, they were always ready to take us along, help us, take our mind off things, give us a good time.

I learned to play the concertina, cook Chinese food, and bring myself to eat fish that had been hooked and gutted before my eyes. Those weekends on the water helped us a lot. They were aids to existence denied to our parents.

During one such weekend, Little Inge had a tragicomic experience:

"It happened in the train from Wedel to Hamburg. I and an equally blonde girlfriend had come straight off the boat and boarded the train in our blue ducks and white summer blouses.

It was sweltering hot, and we'd grabbed two corner seats. The section was jam-packed with yachting cronies and tourists. Suddenly we heard a man say, 'Disgraceful of two BDM girls to go on sitting there while older folk have to stand!' There was a silence. Then my girlfriend's half-Jewish husband cleared his throat and growled, 'Quite right, you BDM girls ought to know better!'

"That was when we still had the courage to joke about things."

Another of Little Inge's reminiscences:

9.18.41:   *Jews are entitled to use . . . public transportation only when there is room for them, but not during rush hours, when even some non-Jewish passengers cannot be accommodated. Jews are restricted to second- and third-class travel and may occupy seats only when no other travelers are standing. (P. 350)*

"We were in a streetcar. My father had to stand on the step. The two of us rode down Mittelweg together, I so perfectly attuned to 'master race' notions with my blonde hair and blue eyes, and my poor, dejected father. I was eager to see what would happen. Nothing at all. One or two fellow passengers eyed us curiously, others sympathetically, but no one said anything or looked aggressive."

We existed in a peculiar limbo, torn between fear, suspense, and curiosity. How else could we have endured life, if not as students of the world around us?

HARASSMENT AND
FOREBODING
(1942)

1.3.42: *In view of the impending final solution of the Jewish
problem, emigration from the Reich by Jews of German nationality and stateless Jews is hereby discon-
tinued. . . . (P. 361)*

The Wannsee Conference, which approved the Final Solution, was held on January 20, 1942.

On July 9, 1942, Little Inge's father received an ominous summons to report to Hartungstrasse with one suitcase and the money for his fare. While en route he managed to write a postcard whose wording implied that it had been smuggled off a train. "We're heading east," it said.

That was the last she ever heard of him.

The first major exodus of deportees from Hamburg in October 1942 was witnessed by my former schoolteacher Elisabeth Flügge. Here is how she recalled one particular incident:

"I happened to be calling on a very refined old lady who had been unable to emigrate because of her frail physical condition and was now languishing in one wretched little room. Suddenly we heard a voice on the stairs: 'Everyone to the assembly center' (the Masonic lodge at Moorweide) 'by eight A.M. tomorrow!' She thereupon begged me to strangle her with a towel. I told her I couldn't do that. I cycled off to see the German Red Cross and the leaders of the Jewish community, but they could only advise me to help her pack. The next day the house was deserted and the front door sealed, but I managed to discover that the old lady had been taken to a home for the aged on Bornplatz, and there she died."

I last saw another ex-teacher of mine, Fräulein Angerstein, not long before the first big raid on Hamburg in 1942. She was very ill—suffering from muscular dystrophy. Her head had retained its normal shape, but her arms were terribly withered. Although she could no longer move her shrunken hands, she consoled herself with the literature she loved so much. Propped up behind a book rest, she would wait patiently for a nurse to come and turn the page for her. I told her about Barbara's birth. These days, she said, she wouldn't wear a swastika pin. . . .

Jews destined for deportation could leave their money to "semirelated" members of the family who were staying behind in Germany, but not to "full Jews," meaning any of their children who had emigrated.

My brother and I were accordingly named as her heirs by our great-aunt, Jenny Rosenmeyer, the last surviving sister of our paternal grandmother and Uncle Adolf Calmann (the doctor who had brought us into the world). Her son Kurt had emigrated to London, her daughter-in-law and the grandchildren to New York. She, being old and sick, could not obtain an entry visa to any foreign country.

We didn't want the money, but Father pointed out that we couldn't touch it anyway because it was held in a blocked account and would remain there for the foreseeable future. This way, he said, there was at least a slender possibility of keeping it in the family.

One afternoon Aunt Jenny telephoned us. "They're sending us off to Theresienstadt," she said in a tremulous voice. "We managed to buy places in a home there." She was then living in an old people's home at or near Blankenese. Little Inge and I went there to say good-bye. Aunt Jenny was braver than either of us, but it was a heartrending farewell.

These "home purchase deeds," I should add, were one of the Nazis' most cynical frauds, because the following decree was absolutely worthless:

6.18.42: *Home purchase deeds are to be prepared for persons who will in the future be deported to Theresienstadt. . . .* P. 377)

Anyone interested in the subject should read Käthe Starke's *Der Führer schenkt den Juden eine Stadt*, published in 1975. How people wound up in Theresienstadt, which was Hitler's attempt to convince foreigners of his humanity, and how they "lived," vegetated, and died there, is a macabre theme in its own right. There were no gas chambers, just starvation and disease and harassment in all its infinitely humiliating forms. For most of the inhabitants, Theresienstadt was a wretched transit camp on the road to extermination.

Aunt Jenny and the other old ladies from her home were assigned to a batch of deportees who never arrived. It later transpired that, in many cases, "gassing vans" were summarily put to work en route.

One tries to find retrospective consolation—if the word can be used here—in the thought that these old and under-nourished people, whose children were already safe overseas, and who dreaded the rigors of the journey ahead, may at least briefly have hoped that Theresienstadt would provide them with a new home in which to await the end of the war and an eventual reunion with their loved ones.

One reason why the infant Federal Republic of Germany made such heavy weather of Aunt Jenny's will was that a testamentary court in Hamburg wanted to pay me and my brother our illegitimate legacies in the early 1950s, even though the legitimate heirs had survived overseas. We managed with some difficulty to put things right, but our cousins across the channel and the Atlantic insisted that we share in their sad inheritance.

1.4.42: *Confidential. Further to the collection of woolens and furs for the eastern front, Jews are to be urged to surrender articles of winter clothing suitable for the front. Elders of resident Jewish communities must be informed that it would cause resentment among citizens of German stock if Jews continued to wear fur garments while citizens of German stock self-sacrificingly donated articles of winter clothing for the front. Jews will be expected to surrender such garments voluntarily, so as to obviate house-to-house searches. (P. 361)*

1.5.42: *Jews who are obliged to wear the Jewish star in public have until 1.16.42 to . . . surrender any fur and woolen garments in their possession. . . . (P. 362)*

These absurd decrees were bad for many reasons, not the least of which was an earlier sentence of hardship passed on the Jews in 1938:

2.14.38: *The minister of economic affairs announces that, in view of prevailing public sentiment, electrical and gas companies*

102

> *need have no qualms about excluding Jews by amending*
> *their statutes. (P. 216)*

This meant that German families wishing to harass Jewish fellow tenants could have their cables and pipes disconnected from the mains and cut off their power and gas supplies.

When we were visited after the war by a lady from Emmendingen who had emigrated to America, she gratefully recalled the kindness of some "Aryan" neighbors. Though unable to prevent her from being disconnected, they had drilled a hole in the floor and lowered an electric lead so that her "Jewish" baby's milk could be heated. That anecdote, too, deserves a place here.

In January 1942—the month of the "eastern front" decrees—my father brought me a fur coat belonging to a Jewish friend of ours. It wasn't an expensive fur, only a black sealskin, but nicely tailored. To me it seemed the height of elegance.

"I'm to tell you you're welcome to it."

I yearned to feel happy about the coat, but I did and I didn't. Spruce and snug, I was walking the wintry, wartime streets at someone else's expense.

Incidental note: it wasn't the soldiers at the front who attired themselves in Jewesses' fur coats. . . .

In the summer of 1942 our friend Ali, who had been drafted into an antiaircraft unit, was burned to death in an air raid on Hamburg.

THE FINAL REUNION
(1943)

10.7.40: *Although Jews cannot in practice be denied the use of air raid shelters, care must be taken to segregate them from the other occupants, either by creating a separate shelter for them, or by partitioning them off. (P. 327)*

A KIND OF MALAISE overcame me on the afternoon of July 24, 1943. I'd been fire-watching the night before, a regulation duty in all Hamburg office buildings, and the first shift hadn't been relieved till midnight. Was that why I felt so exhausted? After work Rolf Sommer took me to the Bodega on Rathausmarkt, where we sat over a glass of wine—a rare treat at that stage of the war—with Dr. Pschorr, his business associate, and Herbert Samuel, his attorney. For the umpteenth time, we debated our current preoccupations—in an undertone, of course. How much longer? Would we make it? Would we survive the bombing and the Gestapo?

My mother asked if I was ill when I got home. I couldn't say, exactly. Was it a presentiment of some kind? Edgy and depressed, I retired to bed early.

We never suspected, when the sirens started wailing, that we would never see our shabby, cozy old apartment again. It went up two terrible hours later, a bare thirty minutes after we quit the cellar. The building had been hit by a delayed-action bomb.

I would be exceeding the scope of my subject if I gave a

detailed description of our last night in the air raid shelter at No. 72, Hansastrasse. Suffice it to say that I sat there with the baby on my lap while my mother toured the two subterranean chambers, radiating confidence and sedating terrified old ladies with tincture of valerian. Every inch a soldier's daughter, I thought, admiring her self-discipline, because she was just as scared as the rest of us. The floor, the walls, the ceilings with their vulnerable maze of gas and water pipes— everything periodically shuddered and shook. From time to time my mother went upstairs to the janitor's apartment, where information and instructions poured in from some civil defense center for as long as the telephone system and radio station continued to function. Curiously enough, the Führer's female devotees—the ones who shared our floor of the house— had never observed or enforced the "segregation" decree. On the contrary, they swallowed my mother's valerian without turning a hair. I wondered what it must feel like to be ministered to by a woman who'd gone to jail because you'd denounced her. . . .

Then came the order to evacuate the building. We made our way in single file along a narrow, subterranean passage, emerged into the street, and headed for Hochallee. Take nothing with you and be quick, we were told. Only the janitor and my mother knew why.

In recounting what happened next, I shall abandon the tone appropriate to a memoir of this kind, which should strive to be impersonal and objective. The following account of my parents' last meeting, every word of which is true, appeared in Freiburg's *Badische Zeitung* as long ago as 1955.

I hurried along Hansastrasse with the baby in my arms, past rows of burning buildings. The whole neighborhood seemed to be ablaze. How in God's name had my father fared in nearby Dillstrasse, I wondered, and where was Wolfgang?

On and on I went, turning occasionally to look for my mother. She was lagging behind, toiling along under the weight of an old woman who was clinging to her and whimpering. Men in dungarees or civil defense corps uniforms stood outside blazing, smoking buildings. They signaled which way we should go by pointing and waving us on. Words would have been inaudible above the hiss and roar of the flames, the wail of ambulance sirens. Barbara's big blue eyes gazed placidly at the incandescent sky. Figures erupted from every door and hurried in our wake. We passed Ingrid's house, but I couldn't tell if it was on fire and didn't know if she and little Kai were still there.

At last the glare faded. Exhausted, I came to a halt. Mother and the old woman soon caught up, and we all perched on a garden wall. Behind us, ash veiled the sky like a gauze curtain. To left and right, seas of flame billowed high into the air. We were outside a corner house in Hochallee, where we used to live. A youngish woman came up to us, and we recognized her as Frau Schenk, our postwoman.

"Our place has a big cellar with emergency exits," she said. "We're laying out some mattresses right now. I'll let you have some proper bedclothes, and you can use my bathroom, too." We couldn't believe our ears!

The cellar was filled with exhausted people. Many were numb with shock, others quietly sobbing. Frau Schenk showed us into a little side room, provided us with bedclothes, brought us bread and steaming mugs of ersatz coffee. She attended to everyone's needs with the same angelic calm and deliberation. Somebody claimed to have heard the all clear in the distance. Our own sirens, which had evidently been destroyed, remained silent.

"I'm going to look for Father," I said, when Mother and Barbara were comfortably installed, and sallied forth into the night. It wasn't far to Dillstrasse, but I had to make several detours. There were signs of confusion everywhere—obstacles, fires, mountains of rubble. Members of the "master race" were accommodated in a concrete shelter nearby. The Jews of Dillstrasse, who were forbidden to set foot in this, had to retire to the cellars of their dilapidated old houses. Not for their own protection, though—far from it. According to the authorities, they had to leave their places of residence during air raids to prevent them from flashing signals to enemy aircraft!

Dillstrasse had been cordoned off. I could hear the shouts of firemen at work and the wail of fire engines racing to the scene, but the street itself was inaccessible. None of the houses had taken a direct hit, I was told, and I had to be content with that.

Frau Schenk was standing wearily outside her door when I returned. "Where on earth have you been?" she demanded. "Haven't you had enough excitement for one night?"

I leaned against the wall beside her. "I've been looking for my father. He lives in—in the neighborhood. My parents are divorced, but they're still on friendly terms."

"Better get some rest," said Frau Schenk. "You've a lot on your shoulders now." Was I wrong, or did I detect some special meaning in her tone? "And tomorrow morning you can go and get your father. Bring him here, then you and your mother won't need to worry so much."

Her kindly suggestion made my stomach turn over. Could we risk it? The Gestapo probably had enough to do without keeping track of us, especially now that our tracks had, in a sense, been obliterated. On the other hand, what if someone in the cellar recognized us? What if some Nazi harridan from the old people's home had found her way there?

Frau Schenk was a mind reader. "You're in the side room, aren't you? Well then! I'll put an extra camp bed in there, so say no more. Now go and get some sleep."

"For God's sake!" said my mother when I told her the wonderful news. "Are you sure it isn't a trap?"

Don't start crying, I told myself. If I started crying now I'd never stop. Our home was gone, but I mustn't cry.

"You only have to look at her," I said, though experience had taught us never to judge by friendly appearances. Even the people who had devised so many torments for us and translated them into law were kind to their friends and families, fed their canaries, fondled their dogs, and played Bach or Brahms. Not Mendelssohn, of course.

The house where my father lived had only had its windows shattered by blast. Plaster had fallen from the ceilings and walls, and the furniture and stacks of newspapers in his room were coated with a thin film of dust. At long last I could indulge in the luxury of a few tears of exhaustion and relief.

"The air raid warden complimented me." My father managed a faint smile. "I was up on the roof, putting out fires."

"Good God!" I exclaimed.

"You forget I'm an old soldier. I've been in action."

"Oh, sure, and you were trying to repay the fatherland for the privilege of climbing out of a Jewish cellar onto an Aryan roof!"

"They were all quite nice to us, the place was in such chaos."

I refrained from commenting on this acme of kindhearted

naïveté. Instead, I told him about Frau Schenk and her proposal. He echoed my mother's question.

"Mightn't it be a trap? I don't know. Just think, though, all of us being together at last. . . . If only Wolfgang would turn up, too!"

Wolfgang would see the ruins of No. 72, Hansastrasse, and assume the worst. Here at Dillstrasse we could only leave a sign of life, not a forwarding address. "I'll leave word at Little Inge's and the office," I said, hoping that nothing had happened to either place.

Wolfgang, who had spent the night at a friend's house, was at Little Inge's when I got there. He was overjoyed, because the sight of the ruins in Hansastrasse had filled him with the direst fears for our safety.

No one looked at us twice as we hurried through Frau Schenk's cellar and into the side room. "I brought you some cigarettes," my father told his divorced wife, as if they had parted only that morning, instead of being so brutally separated at Gestapo headquarters two years before.

He was playing with Barbara all the time. He produced a few cookies from his briefcase, together with a miniature bottle of brandy for me. Only someone aware of how drastically Jewish rations had been cut could gauge what it meant that he had still contrived to bring us each a little present. . . .

If I may be permitted, somewhat emotionally, to sum up this final encounter between my parents, I would put it thus: all their estrangement seemed to have melted away. There was no yesterday, nor would there be any tomorrow. There was just a friendly acceptance of the here and now in a stuffy little room lit not only by a candle whose flame flickered a trifle from lack of oxygen, but also by bright and affectionate memories of a past whose radiance was soon to be extinguished forever.

The next day my boss, Rolf Sommer, took us all to his house in Alsterdorf. From there he drove my mother, Barbara, and me to Lübeck, where we caught a train for the south of Germany. Our friend Olli Cohnheim had contacted us by phone via Little Inge and offered to put us up at her little cottage on the Rothof above Staufen, where peace still reigned.

Wolfgang remained in Hamburg with his girlfriend and wife-to-be. This meant that he was near my father, who went back to the unrelenting wretchedness of the Dillstrasse ghetto. It was typical of Felix Hecht, lawyer and old soldier, that he should have declined to leave the city with the aid of false papers. The authorities could not have checked up on him, at least for some time, but he was mortally afraid of exposing us to *Sippenhaft*, the Nazis' revival of a primitive Germanic law under which an entire family could be punished for the actions of one of its members.

My brother and I are still haunted by the thought that we failed to talk him into going—failed to stand by him like Ingrid, who saw to it that her mother survived the war under the pseudonym "Frau Meier." The loneliness he felt after our departure was only slightly mitigated by Wolfgang's future parents-in-law, who courageously helped him whenever they could.

After the war, when I traveled from Freiburg to Hamburg for a reunion with Wolfgang, the first thing I did was to call on Frau Schenk. It transpired that she had known all about us. "I used to deliver mail to Dillstrasse, too," she explained. "That's why I gave you the side room when you landed up here."

I was almost speechless with gratitude and admiration. "But weren't you scared of helping us like that?"

"Not that I remember," she said. "Everything was in such chaos. Anyway, even if I had been scared, what would my fears have been compared with yours?"

THE WAR YEARS
(1943–1945)

12.18.43: *Jews whose mixed marriages have been dissolved (hitherto exempted from wearing the Jewish star) and persons of formal Jewish status [Geltungsjuden] are to be sent to Theresienstadt. (P. 401)*

I SHUTTLED TO AND FRO between Staufen and Hamburg until Rolf Sommer evacuated his firm from the battered city to Marktredwitz, in Bavaria. He was going to let me know when his business had been allocated premises large enough to accommodate me, too. Instead, I was notified as follows:

"10.16.43. I regret to inform you that I cannot employ you for the time being. My reasons can only be communicated by word of mouth. . . ."

Dr. Pschorr received an identical letter. Sommer's Nazi clerk had stepped up the pressure. . . .

So I was unemployed. Herr Ilch, the mayor of Staufen, refrained from questioning me too closely. Although he was a Party member, he allowed me to do secretarial work at the town hall. They knew me there because I was always borrowing back numbers of the *Staufener Wochenblätter* from Herr Dufner, the town clerk. These contained articles on local history that I used as aids to familiarize myself with my new, adopted home.

We had managed, after making one or two detours, to

acquire a haven in the old granary on Marktplatz: one large room which we divided into two with wardrobes and closets. There was no running water—that we had to fetch from a fountain in Freihofgasse, opposite the side entrance—but we did have two handsome tiled stoves. My mother had learned how to stoke small cast-iron stoves during our stay with Olli on the Rothof, but tiled stoves? Although we were assigned a ration of logs, these were dumped in Freihofgasse, a narrow alleyway, and had to be split and toted upstairs. There was a chopping block on the Marktplatz side, but my vain attempts to wield an ax must have looked so pathetic that Emil Gutmann, another of the town hall clerks, put a stop to them. He solved our problem in short order by splitting the logs himself and teaching us how to stoke the stoves properly. It so happened that the OG, or local Party boss, lived on the top floor of the town hall, so he could see what was going on in the medieval marketplace below. One day he gave vent to the following pronouncement: "Fancy a German and a Party member chopping wood for a *Jewess* with a Party-owned ax!"

Fortunately, the OG never did more than attack us verbally—for instance to Fräulein Gysler, who owned the Freihof facing the granary. A fine old building designed by Peter Thumb, the celebrated eighteenth-century architect, the Freihof had once enjoyed the right of asylum. Fräulein Gysler, who still took this seriously, offered us shelter in its stout cellars when Allied aircraft flew over the little town, as they did with increasing frequency. Evidently conversant with the segregation order, the OG urged her to exclude us from her protection. Fräulein Gysler refused point-blank. She was a loyal German, she told him, but she didn't equate loyalty with inhumanity. It wasn't until much later that I learned of this courageous retort.

Where the treatment of "half-breeds" was concerned, the

authorities had exhibited differences of opinion as early as 1935. They were uncertain of our place in the scale of racial values, which may explain why no proceedings were taken against me on account of Barbara's birth. As time went by, however, interpretations of the Nuremberg Laws increased in stringency until, by the end of 1943, the outlook for partners in mixed marriages and for us, their children, was extremely ominous. Alois Schnorr, a Staufen bank manager who subsequently became finance minister of the little state of Baden, was arrested not long before the war ended. His Jewish wife was hidden by friends; his "half-breed" children were ostracized in the school playground by order of their teacher, Herr F., who also happened to be the aforesaid local Party boss.

Back in Hamburg, my father paid sporadic, halfhearted visits to the Honduran consulate to inquire about the current immigration quota.

On January 18, 1944, he gave my brother a handwritten postcard: "I hereby assign my son, Wolfgang Hecht of Hamburg 13 . . . power of attorney. This entitles him to take all requisite steps in my behalf. It shall not be rendered void by my death. Dr. Felix Israel Hecht." He had received his dread summons.

Neither of them let us know. Wolfgang didn't call Staufen until the train had departed on its sinister journey. He had escorted Father to the Talmud Torah School on Grindelhof and left him there with sixty other companions in misfortune. They were the fifteenth batch of deportees from Hamburg. Their destination: Theresienstadt.

Until 1942 we had never even heard of this former Austro-Hungarian fortress in Czechoslovakia, midway between Dresden and Prague. Now, its name was to be imprinted on our memories forever.

4.5.42: *Police commissioners, district administrators, and mayors of the Lower Rhine area are instructed not to enter the destination of consignments [of deportees] in their records. They are simply to mark them "Gone away, whereabouts unknown" or "Emigrated." (P. 369)*

This monstrous though altogether logical directive probably applied to the inmates of Theresienstadt as well, but at least their relatives received news of them. Theresienstadt was a deportation center that the Nazis used in an attempt to feign humane treatment of the Jews, principally for the benefit of foreigners. Foreign delegations were admitted, though their visits were stage-managed to a degree that put Potemkin's villages in the shade.

My father sent his first card from Berlin: "Dear children, everything has gone uneventfully so far. We're due to arrive about seven. Then we'll have to wait and see what happens." At Theresienstadt he met up with his sister Aunt Alice, who had been there since 1942 with her charges from the old people's home in Berlin.

The town was still divided into grid squares when my father got there. Street names were added later, so his "L 6" became Wallstrasse and "L 3" was christened Lange Strasse. To prevent the development of even a semblance of settled existence, no one was allowed to "live" in the same place for very long. The cold, bleak barrack rooms were usually crammed with people, all of whom had just as much space as their physical stature required. The boundaries of these "ubications" were staked out with their belongings, in other words, a suitcase and a heap of clothes.

Slightly more space was allotted to elderly men who had once made a special contribution to the life of the country that now disowned them. Academics for the most part, they were privileged to share one largish room with several of their number.

Although deportees were forbidden to receive "money and gift parcels of any description," there were many things that could be sent to Theresienstadt. We had little enough to send, however, and the preprinted reply cards were tersely worded: "Theresienstadt,____1944. I gratefully acknowledge receipt of your parcel dated____1944. Signed____."

Inmates were permitted to preface these cards with the words "My dear" (or something similar) and add postscripts such as "I'm well—the jam and potatoes tasted wonderful" or "Very thoughtful of you to put in some shoe polish and shoe-laces." The latter were disguised requests, and we responded at once by sending off jam and potatoes, shoe polish and shoe-laces. Parcels being subject to a weight limit, the amount of food that could be sent—potatoes, for example—was pitifully small but vitally important nonetheless. When my father wrote under another name, as he did from time to time, we knew that a fellow deportee with no family had bequeathed him his monthly mail ration.

It was sometimes possible to write at greater length: "June 1, 1944 . . . Thank you first of all for the parcels, which have been arriving almost daily of late. I was very pleased with the contents, especially the rolled oats and the onions. They arrived safely because they were securely wrapped and strung. I can well believe that Barbara is progressing and endearing herself to everyone as much as you say. Inge is quite at liberty to enclose a picture of the child in her letter. She'll be three in August, so her little face must have changed a great deal. . . ."

On July 14, 1944, we received a card signed "Lutz Helischkowsky." It read: "Wolfgang's parcels of lard and canned vegetables arrived safely. Aunt Alice is managing all our cooking very well. She's still working for the health service, just as Pappi is still working as a lawyer. He has also taken over the running of a library, which suits him perfectly, as you can imagine, and gives him special pleasure. The weather here has been mostly fine. Apart from *Tosca* . . . we've been to a dress rehearsal of *Cyrano de Bergerac* and heard a lovely Mozart piano concerto, also some scenes from Ibsen's *Nora* and *The Lady from the Sea*. . . ."

Sometimes, for self-defensive reasons, we allowed ourselves to be lulled into a false sense of security by glowing reports of this kind. Opera? Concerts? Plays? The explanation emerges from Käthe Starke's book on Theresienstadt. Most performances like the ones mentioned—recreational activities pursued by people living in hopeless isolation but reluctant to abandon hope—were laboriously cobbled together by scholars who had filled their baggage with books instead of the practical necessities of life; either that, or enthusiasts combed the libraries, of which there were several, for musical scores and theatrical scripts. The *Cyrano*, for instance, was just a play reading which "for various Theresienstadt reasons" never got beyond the rehearsal stage.

We didn't dare publicize our connection with Theresienstadt, so Wolfgang used to forward Father's postcards in sealed envelopes. At first we naïvely believed that no one in Staufen would ever discover our personal circumstances. I now know how our particulars found their way so promptly to Gestapo headquarters at Lörrach. They were sent there in compliance with a directive issued long before the war:

9.6.35: *A Jewish file is to be opened, covering all Jews throughout Germany. (P. 126)*

Our identification was child's play, therefore, and made even easier by a subsequent, additional request from Gestapo headquarters at Karlsruhe:

11.6.40: *Secret State Police [Gestapo] offices are instructed to keep a record of Jews and half-breeds. (Three files: full Jews, first degree half-breeds, and persons of German blood professing the Jewish faith.) (P. 329)*

I mentioned that we had to make one or two detours before settling down in the old granary. There we could do as we pleased, but the same could not be said of our previous quarters. We'd had to be very discreet for the sake of a landlady who accommodated my mother and Barbara in the town, thereby sparing them a long and arduous trek from the Rothof, which stood in mountainous seclusion. We shall never forget the political courage she displayed in accepting us as lodgers. At the same time, we did have to contend with certain other difficulties that made it necessary for us to find a summer retreat somewhere outside town. A friendly family named Bob had a tennis pavilion and swimming pool in the middle of the verdant Etzenbach Valley, and this they put at our disposal. The "pavilion" was just a shack containing one small, oval room and a cellar. We often moved the local inhabitants to laughter by disappearing into the cellar at the first sound of aircraft, even though we realized that this small repository for tennis rackets would protect us from splinters at most. They stopped laughing after February 8, 1945, when the little town was devastated by Allied fighter bombers.

We spent many happy hours in the shack, I painting tiles and bookmarks, my mother manufacturing rather shapeless dolls out of old stockings and scraps of material. They all found a ready market, and I built up a faithful clientele among the stationers of Freiburg, who had no fountain pens or writing paper left to sell.

To refugees from a bomb-blasted city, the Etzenbach Valley was pure delight. We drank in the Black Forest air with gratitude, well aware of our good fortune. Then, one day, we were spotted by the OG, who kept his beehives nearby. There was something ominous about his habit of peering across at us. "He's got the evil eye," I said, and I was right. Friendly neighbors advised us not to provoke him by parading our cheerful, unconstrained existence before his eyes. Our move to the granary came none too soon.

This, incidentally, was around the time when the "September consignments" left Theresienstadt for Auschwitz, but of that we were still in ignorance. We merely wondered, with deep foreboding, why the flow of postcards had abruptly ceased.

On April 5, 1944, my brother Wolfgang was drafted for forced labor.

On October 10, 1950, the Hamburg Reparations Office declined to pay him compensation for wrongful imprisonment, a legal entitlement, on the ground that "no deprivation of liberty akin to imprisonment can be ascertained." Wolfgang commented on the decision to Herbert Samuel, who was representing him, in a letter dated March 28, 1951:

"Setting aside this very flimsy argument, it is unjustifiable and contrary to the spirit of the law to reject my claim while approving those of sundry acquaintances who worked alongside me in the same detachment. I realize that courts in various places have arrived at contrary conclusions in the same matter, but I feel that such things should not be allowed to happen in these reparation cases."

We often wondered, as the years went by and reparation proceedings dragged on, where and how the officials author-

124

ized to rule on such cases had lived during the Third Reich. . . . In Wolfgang's case the ruling was reversed on November 26, 1951, after he had submitted the following account of his experiences:

"Our so-called liability to forced labor was merely part of an extermination campaign, as the records of the Central State Security Bureau prove beyond doubt. . . . We had to assemble every morning in the gymnasium at Altona, where we were detailed for duty by squad commanders v. H. and B. I was in District 7. After morning parade . . . we were assigned work and had to march to the site in detachments, sometimes guarded by uniformed SA men. Our work consisted exclusively of strenuous manual labor, to which I and many of my friends were quite unaccustomed. I had been drafted from Glassmanufaktur Paul Besser of Altona, where I was a trainee clerk. We were paid the lowest possible wage (an unskilled laborer's rate) and were not entitled to . . . vacations or accident insurance . . . nor to any free time. We had to be on call day and night, and were obliged to report to Altona immediately after every air raid on Hamburg, nights and Sundays included. I spent many Sundays on duty, performing the following tasks: salvaging girders; demolishing buildings; retrieving corpses; carrying furniture and utensils out of bomb-damaged houses; stringing up power cables; repairing water mains; unearthing mains by shoring up bomb craters in snow and rain; salvaging bomb-damaged machinery; shoring up walls (at the risk of our lives, because hardly any of us knew how to handle girders or machinery without bringing rubble down on us); shoveling coal; emptying ashcans; and constructing antitank ditches with . . . prisoners of war and concentration camp detainees.

"The following quirk of fate may serve to illustrate our sense of insecurity. We had been detailed to dig some antitank ditches just beyond Harburg with a detachment of some ten Germans and sixty Italian prisoners of war. Five of my comrades were distraught because they had been ordered, out of the blue, to report the next day to a camp at Harburg-Wilhelmsburg commanded by a then notorious SS officer. We were in a state of utter consternation, because that meant being confined to barracks. Toward midday, Harburg sustained a severe and unheralded air raid. Not being accommodated in an air raid shelter, we and the prisoners spent the entire raid lying in the open between two antiaircraft batteries, which were later blown to pieces. We reached the construction site after marching for hours, and had occasion to note that the said camp had also been destroyed in the raid. . . .

"Because of my inexperience at lifting heavy weights, I developed tendinitis of the right hand, among other things. I was recalled two weeks later and assigned to District 1 soon afterward. I now had to parade every morning on Hegeplatz in Eppendorf under the command of G., a paver. At first the work was the same as before, but we later had to spend part of the time in Gross-Borstel PW camp, where we were put to work with Polish prisoners of war. The work there was generally more dangerous than in District 7, because we were employed in Harburg-Wilhelmsburg during heavy raids and not allowed to take cover when the early warning siren sounded. Most of our workplaces were fifteen or twenty minutes away from the shelters, so we nearly always got caught up in the raids. Air raid wardens several times refused to admit us to shelters on account of the Polish prisoners. In the case of the Wilhelmsburg surface shelter, in particular, we often had to dash inside during the panic that ensued on the dropping of the first bombs.

"I more than once worked twenty-two hours out of twenty-four at Harburg, where we had to repair railroad tracks in spite of continual explosions from the duds strewn around the oil refineries. . . . When sweeping streets and emptying ash-cans, we had to report to a square near Haynstrasse, where we were detailed to assist employees of the Public Sanitation Service. Discounting the few assignments that enabled us to render people genuine assistance by digging them out of cellars or salvaging their possessions, the whole of our compulsory service was harassment, pure and simple, and we were powerless to resist our supervisors' oft-reiterated intention to 'put us where we belonged.'

"We were discharged on April 24, 1945. . . . I survived this spell of heavy manual labor relatively unscathed, except for a deteriorating knee injury. What I found worst of all was the constant mental strain and uncertainty. . . ."

My brother's knee injury still troubles him to this day. He ought to walk a good deal, having suffered a minor cardiac infarction, but it precludes him from doing so.

One of Wolfgang's fellow conscripts was Herbert Samuel, our attorney friend, and his first meeting with Ralph Giordano—they were both born in 1923—also dates from this period. Like Wolfgang, Giordano describes the parades on Hegeplatz, characterizing Herbert as a "once-prominent lawyer of the Free and Hanseatic City of Hamburg" who urged all present to maintain discipline and "comply with all instructions issued by those in authority over them."

Herbert Samuel, a universally respected figure, died on April 16, 1982. Wolfgang, who now lives in Latin America, described him in a letter to me as "a link with the past, and one of the last people to have known and been associated with our family's fate from early on." He also recalled: "When our squad commander greeted us in the morning with 'Heil Hitler,' Sammi's lone voice could be heard replying, 'And a very good morning to *you*. . . .' "

On January 2, 1952, Wolfgang was awarded compensation of DM 1,800 for wrongful imprisonment. In other words, his wages of fear amounted to DM 150 a month.

On February 7, 1945, I had to undergo an emergency operation in Freiburg while the hospital was under threat from low-flying aircraft. Though still very weak, I was sent home far too soon. The reasons for this were numerous and compelling. On February 8 the little town of Staufen sustained a heavy air raid that killed eighty of its inhabitants and destroyed forty houses. Blast had shattered the granary's windows and toppled our bookshelves. Everything was thick with dust—to our eyes, a familiar sight! My mother, who had been forced to neglect a bad bout of bronchitis, spent most of the time with Barbara in Fräulein Gysler's cellar across the way, relying on neighbors to cook for her. Things could hardly have been worse.

A Gestapo officer from Lörrach appeared on my first night home. Darkness had already fallen when we heard his boots come clumping up the stairs. He knocked loudly and demanded to speak to me. My mother swayed and leaned against the wall, assailed by memories of her time in Fuhlsbüttel Prison. I couldn't stand straight, far less walk. The man announced that I had been drafted, but my physical condition was obvious, and I also had a note from the hospital authorities certifying that they'd had to discharge me prematurely.

"I'll be back," the man said.

"Why?" I asked. "I'm the offspring of a privileged mixed marriage. That makes me half-Aryan."

The look he gave me was as unforgettable as his reply. "Half-Aryan? Half-Jewish, you mean, and that's as good as Jewish. Jews and Negroes, they're all the same to me." Then, "I'll order you to Lörrach three weeks from now."

"He forgot about the gypsies," I said when he'd gone,

recalling one of the by-products of the "blood preservation" law:

12.19.35:   *The only races in Europe to be regarded as alien are Jews and gypsies. (P. 146)*

So terror had stalked us to Staufen. Herr Dufner confided to me the next day that the Gestapo officer had called once before, but that he, Dufner, had "acted dumb."

I might have escaped the Lörrach authorities by setting off for Hamburg, but I was far too weak to travel. Besides, I couldn't risk abandoning my mother and child to their barbaric notions of collective responsibility, so I stayed put. Three weeks later the gentlemen of the Gestapo had other things on their minds. As in Hamburg, so in Lörrach, they were doubtless busy destroying their files.

French troops entered Staufen on April 23, 1945, my mother's forty-fifth birthday. From that day on, the invisible walls that had been erected between us and "the others" could be gradually dismantled.

Gradually, but not easily.

Fear dogged Little Inge, too, to the very last.

"July 1944, shortly before the birth of my son Thomas, who was due in August . . . I heard on the twentieth that an attempt had been made on Hitler's life, and for a few short hours I hoped that everything would be safely over by the time the child arrived. . . . But it went on.

"After the baby was born, my days in the hospital were haunted by a constant fear of questions—Who's the father? Why aren't you married?—but the deaconesses at the Bethesda asked me nothing. Their manner was reassuringly affable and discreet.

"One of the many problems awaiting me was potentially lethal. When registering the child's birth, I would have to produce my own birth certificate, which showed that I was a *Geltungsjüdin* [officially Jewish], not a 'first degree half-breed,' because my mother had adopted the Jewish faith on her marriage.

"Under the law, I should have worn a star and been sent to Theresienstadt. So far, for some reason, my status had remained undetected because I was 'racially' no different from the so-called 'privileged half-breeds,' especially as I had been baptized with Big Inge in 1938. Having received a final notice to register the child, I went to the registry office early in February. I claimed that my birth certificate had been destroyed in an air raid—a bold assertion, because we had never been bombed out. The registrar, who seemed friendly enough, made a note of my (false) particulars. Two weeks later I received a summons from the Gestapo to bring them my 'Aryan certificate.' I was interviewed by a woman official. Just as I entered her office, she was called away for a few moments. I managed to peek at the folder lying open on her desk. It turned out that the 'friendly' registrar had consulted his files and reported me. I was curtly informed that I was a *Geltungsjüdin*, knew what that implied, and would be notified in due course. That could only have meant a deportation order. Alarming though the prospect was, I decided to take the baby and make a dash for the Allied lines. I had spun out the proceedings long enough, however, because at the end of February the Gestapo authorities in Hamburg started destroying their records. The British were very near by then, so I and my baby were spared the appalling fate that overtook so many 'half-breeds' just before the Nazi regime came to an end."

AFTERWARD . . .

THE NAZIS' LEGAL SUCCESSORS found us rather difficult to deal with. We found them even more so.

Hamburg had been occupied by the British, Staufen by the French. Although Wolfgang was unable to get his apartment in Harvestehude exempted from seizure—the British requisitioned whole streets and blocks—the French authorities proved quite amenable. The biggest problem we had to contend with for a while was an order to return to Hamburg. What, after all, would we have done there?

In 1948 I married and settled in Badenweiler, so my long and laborious struggle to stay put was over at last.

For Wolfgang, life after the liberation was harder. Week after week he went to meet the buses returning from Theresienstadt, but our father was never on board.

We later consulted one of the bodies set up to deal with the innumerable cases like ours. In 1948, three years after the end of the war, we received a communication from the Missing Persons Service of the VVN or Vereinigung der Opfer des Naziregimes [Association of Victims of the Nazi Regime]:

"Re Dr. Felix Hecht, b. 9.24.83 in Hamburg.

"Having consulted Prague on the subject of the above inquiry, we today received the following reply: 'Pursuant to your inquiry of 4.9.47, we inform you that the lists of our Evidence Bureau contain this note on the above-mentioned person: "Dr. Felix Hecht, b. 9.24.83 in Hamburg, last place of residence Hamburg, was . . . transferred to Auschwitz (from Theresienstadt) with Consignment Ev 1651." Persons aged fifty and over may be regarded as deceased.'

"We regret our inability to give you any other reply."

Wolfgang decided to emigrate and now, as I have already said, lives in Latin America. His first port of call—a somewhat macabre coincidence—was Honduras. Because he finds the act of recollection unendurable, he has tried to overcome the past by devoting himself to the present. He, after all, came closer to the Final Solution than I: it was he who accompanied our father to the assembly center and was obliged to leave him there. . . .

Reparation . . . For us, this dreadful word has never acquired full meaning because we were only—to employ yet another official term that we had to learn and comprehend—"indirectly prejudiced."

We embarked on a nightmare journey through the jungle of the reparation laws. The authorities, who were obviously overtaxed, overtaxed us in turn. (They still do, by the way!) Every aspect of the "indirect prejudice" we had so patiently suffered had to be proved and proved again—and again. The postcards from Theresienstadt were not enough. Neither was the declaration of death, nor were the notorious "Special Laws." The authorities insisted on letters, testimonials, and affidavits covering every last detail.

Among those who confirmed that I could and would have

134

passed my university entrance examination was Hans Wolff-heim, who had finally, in 1946, obtained a lectureship at Hamburg University. He amplified his official affidavit in 1956—that is how long it all dragged on—by writing to me as follows:

"It is true that half-Jews could matriculate on paper and under the 'law' until 1941, and the bureaucrats of our democratic system appear to take their cue from these regulations. The actual position was quite different, however. There is now a reluctance to acknowledge that everyone, from schools and their principals upward, was at pains to impress the Party authorities as being 'pure Aryan.' Woe betide any half-Jew who invoked the 'law'!"

I got the education grant provided by law, and Wolfgang and I were jointly awarded our father's legal damages for wrongful imprisonment. Calculated from the date of his deportation to his putative date of death, May 1945, these amounted to DM 150 for every month he spent in custody.

To demand proof of our father's loss of earnings would have been absurd, but we had at least to obtain affidavits to the effect that we had lived in comfortable circumstances until 1933. On July 5, 1954, our erstwhile lodger in Hagedornstrasse, Dr. Weil, sent the Reparations Office a letter from London. Part of it read:

"You must know as well as I do that most attorneys from 'good' Hamburg Jewish families derived a substantial income from their practices. . . . As the son of a well-known antique dealer, Dr. Hecht must have been on a really sound financial footing. . . ."

My former employer Emil Todtmann wrote: "My wife, who paid them several visits in their apartment, could tell from the way it was furnished that the H. family must have been well off before 1933."

And so on and so forth, from one indignity to another.

On the subject of Barbara's birth, the Reparations Office received a letter from Wolfgang's group leader in the Paulusbund, Gerhard Wundermacher: "Women who could not marry in consequence of the 'Nuremberg Laws' are among those who suffered most. It may be in the nature of things that no reparation law takes account of the injury they sustained."

In Little Inge's case the Reparations Office came up with another bright idea, though her attorney managed to knock it on the head. Two days after her father's deportation in July 1942, she received a postcard from him, as I have already mentioned. In calculating the amount of compensation due to her, the office wanted to equate the date on the card with the date of his death!

We were stripped of our rights, denied the opportunity to train for worthwhile professions, prevented from building up a livelihood, forbidden to marry. We shared the fears of those who failed to survive persecution, but we also had to endure the shame of having fared better than our fathers, our relations, our friends.

We did not emerge unscathed.

DATE			
APR 29 1988			